D0891489

This book may be kept

A

GEORGE E. BERKLEY
is Assistant Professor of Political Science
at Northeastern University.
Former Chairman of the Boston Finance Commission,
he has written several books and articles on changes
in the nature of American government and business.

George E. Berkley

THE
ADMINISTRATIVE
REVOLUTION

Notes on the Passing of
Organization Man

Prentice-Hall, Inc. Englewood Cliffs, N. J.

A SPECTRUM BOOK

To
Robert R. Robbins,
who believed in delayed vocations

Current printing (last number):

10 9 8 7 6 5 4 3 2 1

PRENTICE-HALL INTERNATIONAL, INC. (*London*)
PRENTICE-HALL OF AUSTRALIA, PTY. LTD. (*Sydney*)
PRENTICE-HALL OF CANADA, LTD. (*Toronto*)
PRENTICE-HALL OF INDIA PRIVATE LIMITED (*New Delhi*)
PRENTICE-HALL OF JAPAN, INC. (*Tokyo*)

37-524

ACKNOWLEDGMENTS

I am first of all indebted to the Department of Political Science at Northeastern University and its chairman, R. Gregg Wilfong, for allowing me a workload that would permit me to write this book. I am also grateful to my colleagues, in particular Professor David Barkley and Assistant Professor James Medeiros, for their numerous kindnesses and help while the manuscript was being prepared. However, a large university has numerous intellectual resources and I was fortunate in being able to call on assistance from others as well. Among these are Lyman A. Keith, Chairman of the Department of Management, Philip R. MacDonald, Associate Professor of Marketing, and Frederick Dunbar, Instructor in Economics. I have also benefited from talks with Assistant Professor Stanley Klein of the University of Massachusetts, Associate Professor Henry A. Selby of the University of Texas, Charles Tenney of Arthur D. Little, and Allen Schick and Graeme M. Taylor of the Brookings Institute. None of these persons has read the manuscript, however, and all should be held blameless for any inaccuracies or controversial opinions contained within it.

Finally, my thanks go out to Miss Margaret E. O'Leary whose excellent typing skills made my task ever so much easier.

CONTENTS

Jedes Leben sei zu fuhren,
Wenn man sich nicht selbst vermisst
Alles konne man verlieren
Wenn man bliebe, was man ist.

—GOETHE

And how many ideas there have been on earth in the history of mankind which were unthinkable ten years before they appeared? Yet, when their distinct hour had come, they came forth and spread over the whole earth. So it will be with us and our people will shine forth in the world, and all men will say, "the stone which the builders rejected has become the cornerstone of the building."

—DOSTOYEVSKY

INTRODUCTION

In May 1962, John F. Kennedy and Andre Malraux lunched together at the Presidential estate in Glen Ora. According to Arthur Schlesinger, the two men "fell into a discussion of the persistence of mythology in the contemporary World. 'In the nineteenth century,' Malraux said, 'the ostensible issue within the European states was the monarchy versus the Republic. But the real issue was capital vs. the proletariat. In the twentieth century the ostensible issue is capital vs. the proletariat. But the World has moved on. What is the real issue now?' The real issue today, Kennedy replied, was the management of industrial society —a problem, he said not of ideology but of administration."

This provocative interchange between two of our century's more provocative figures raises many more questions than it answers. First, was Kennedy correct in suggesting that the long and bitter conflict between employers and employed has now passed from the ideological arena? If so, has the new problem area, the administration of industrial society, generated yet another new area of conflict? And, if so, can and will this new conflict be resolved?

This book is an attempt to answer these questions.

It takes as its theme the fading out of the capital versus labor conflict in society and the emergence in its place of a new troublesome issue: the organization versus the individual. To some extent, of course, this new conflict provides the same battle lines as the old one, but with the opposing ranks broadened to include, on one side, nonprofit as well as profit organizations, and, on the other side, nonproletarians as well as proletarians. However, as Malraux noted, the world moves on. It is now moving on at a faster pace than ever before. Organizations and

1

individuals are both changing and the pattern of change taking place indicates that this conflict is also getting ready to pass from the scene. Convergence is replacing divergence in the management of post-industrial society.

The administrative revolution is only in its beginning stages. It will probably not encompass all the organizational areas of our society for a long, long time. Some institutions may remain comparatively unaffected for decades. Furthermore, like all revolutions, it will probably overshoot its mark and deliver less than it currently promises. However, an administrative revolution is in the making, it does seem destined to gather increasing steam, and it does offer the prospect of drastically modifying if not abolishing the organizational ills which now beset our increasingly organized society.

This administrative upheaval is affecting both the public and private sector, and this book attempts to assess its impact in both areas. The linking of public and private organizations involves some occasional awkwardness since differences between them still remain. To some extent, this study may be guilty of the charge which Ben Johnson flung at the metaphysical poets of his day, that of yoking heterogeneous ideas by violence together. However, the divergences between public and private organizations themselves are diminishing all the time. Business is assuming an increasingly public character while government is making ever more use of business methods and approaches. This growing convergence itself forms part of the Administrative Revolution.

1

THE RISE AND FALL OF BUREAUCRACY

Some years ago an author wrote a book on prostitution entitled *The World's Oldest Profession*. While the title was catchy, it was also erroneous. The world's oldest profession is administration.

The practice of administration is of such ancient vintage that it predates the advent of man himself. The ants, who achieved their current level of evolutionary development some 20 million years ago, provide a compelling picture of administration in action. Their systematic way of dividing and coordinating their efforts could fill a modern-day bureaucrat with awe and wonder.

Higher up the evolutionary ladder we find another example of fine-honed administration in the animal kingdom. These are the beavers who possess a calm disposition and a high capacity to work cooperatively. The dams they build often last for years and, if need be, one can be repaired in a single night.

Our attitudes toward these two animal administrators tell us something about man's relationship to administration. We tend to view the activity of the ant with feelings akin to revulsion and horror. When we compare an organization to an ant hill we are scarcely bestowing praise. Yet, we often regard the cooperative endeavors of the beaver with approval and even admiration. The phrase "busy as a beaver" rings with a positive tone. These contrasting attitudes reflect the ambivalence with which man himself has always reacted toward administration. He continually tends to call for more administrative efficiency in the organizations he deals with while, at the same time, he continually harbors fears that they may become too ruthlessly effective. France's famed Cardinal Richelieu may have had such concerns in mind when he cautioned his administrators "above all, not too much zeal."

Despite such fears and misgivings, however, man has always lived in an administered society. In the beginning there was the family. Later, there was the kinship tribe. Compared with today's full-blown administrative state, administration in those times was much more personal. However, it was also much more coercive. The rules and regulations governing savage society were both extensive and rigid and the penalties for disobedience could be extremely severe. The misty-eyed nostalgia with which modern man tends to conjure up his primitive past does not square with the findings of anthropologists. The supposedly noble and carefree savage generally operated under a system of organizational restraints which makes life in the most bureaucratic of modern-day establishments look like a paradise of anarchy.

Eventually, tribal society gave way to more organized social structures and administration followed suit. Formal public administration as we know it today first appeared thousands of years ago in Mesopotamia. This ancient community felt a pressing need for irrigation and in order to meet this need, it developed a managerial group to divide the work. Some men were assigned to build the necessary canals while others were given the task of growing enough food to feed both the canal builders and themselves. It was thus the appearance of formalized administrative practice which brought civilization onto the world scene.

The early Babylonian, Egyptian, and Chinese civilizations developed a fairly high degree of organizational and managerial effectiveness. The pyramids of Egypt attest to this. Some of these early civilizations even produced writing on administrative problems which show that the basic questions which the subject poses have not changed greatly through the ages.

Ancient China is particularly interesting in this respect. China had developed a rather extensive administrative structure by 1000 B.C. It consisted essentially of a network of lords. Each lord had under him one or more intendants, depending on the size of the lord's domain. Under each intendant functioned a superintendent of forests and cultivated lads, a supervisor of roads and bridges, a chief of engineers, a controller of merchants, a judge, a keeper of prisoners, and an official to look after the horses required for military undertakings.

Many of the country's ancient thinkers were administrative functionaries. However, this did not prevent them from giving early voice to the disquiet which the administration of government has nearly always evoked. Chung-tzu, who lived around 300 B.C. is said to have written a book of wit and charm stating that since happiness can only be achieved by the free development of man's nature, the best method of governing is nongovernment! Mo Ti, a contemporary of Confucius, anticipated William James and the scientific management schools by 2½ millennia in stipulating that institutions should meet a basic pragmatic test: did they benefit society?

Confucius looked to wise and judicious administration by well-qualified men as a way of rescuing his people from their misery and oppression. He sought all his life for a high administrative post so that he could put his ideas into practice. Given the nature of his intentions, it is not surprising that no ruler was moved to grant his wish. As is so often the case, however, the Chinese sage's ideas began to gather influence after his death. The emerging strength of the Emperor vis-a-vis the local lords facilitated this trend. During the Han dynasty (202 B.C.-A.D. 221) it became customary to select ministers on the basis of their personal qualities and not simply on the basis of their ancestry. It even became possible, though by no means easy, for a man of humble birth to rise to the commanding heights of the Chinese Empire. One Han emperor, Wu Ti, established an academy for training public officials and ordered his local subalterns to recommend their best men for its student body.

In the West, the first stirrings of what we now regard as bureaucracy appeared during Roman times. The emergence of two concepts marked this development. One was the view that rulers should derive their powers from the people. The other was the notion that the public purse had an identity and an existence that was separate from the ruler's personal fortune. These two concepts were sometimes more honored in the breach than in the observance—a phenomenon that occasionally occurs even today—but their appearance launched the trend to depersonalized governmental power. This trend was to culminate many centuries later in the advent of the modern bureaucratic state.

To administer their far-flung empire, Roman rulers even began to adopt certain bureaucratic devices such as the delegation of power. Diocletian, for example, reorganized the Roman world into twelve large divisions and appointed a deputy for each. Our modern word "diocese" derives from the term he applied to these territorial units. He also moved to separate military from civil administration with the aim of achieving improved efficiency. He further instituted a limited right of appeal whereby a citizen from an outlying province could, under certain circumstances, bring a grievance against his district administrator to Rome.

During the later days of the Empire, administration reached new levels of development and complexity. The state created and filled such positions as chamberlain, chief judicial and law enforcement officer, war minister, and clerk of state. Still more important for the future was the development of a unified, coherent, and impersonal body of law. Consequently, by the time the Roman Empire had passed into history, it had, in one form or another and at one time or another, germinated such bureaucratic features as chain of command, centralized direction, table of organization, specialization, formalization, and standardization of rules and regulations.

When the lights went out in Rome and the Western World passed into the Dark Ages, these modern-day administrative attributes also went into eclipse. Written law gave way to oral law as well as to law based on custom. Organized administration yielded to personal power founded on personal qualities and personal loyalties. Political power itself became fragmented and centralization disappeared from government. However, many of these concepts received fresh impetus elsewhere through the growth of the Roman Catholic Church. Indeed, the church kept alive many of these Roman achievements in administration, in a sense nurturing them for the day they would later re-emerge.

And re-emerge they did with the rise of the nation-state in the 16th and 17th centuries. The new state gradually assumed functions that were more extensive than those discharged by the Roman Empire. Soon, it gave birth to a new administrative device which was to grow Topsy-like right down to the present. This was the committee. The first of these committees was the privy council which consisted of the King and his royal secretaries. The privy council was a forerunner of our modern-day cabinet. France, for example, by the middle of the 16th century had, in embryonic form, a foreign secretary, a minister of interior, a minister of war, a minister of marine affairs, a chancellor, and a comptroller general.

As we scan the growth of administration in the modern era, we notice a rather interesting and somewhat unexpected trend. Many of those leaders who based their rule most completely on the force of their personalities introduced measures which, at the same time, reduced the role of personality in government. Louis the XIV of France and Peter the Great of Russia both tightened, and, in a sense, depersonalized the administrative structures of their separate countries. In the 18th century, Frederick the Great put Prussia into the vanguard of administrative development by introducing considerable centralization and establishing a corps of professional public servants based largely on a merit system. Napoleon set up the prefectoral corps which still runs France today.

By the middle of the 19th century, the revived and expanded Roman concept of the state having an existence distinct from that of the individuals who ran it reached its full flower. As Brian Chapman has put it, the public official "became a instrument of public power and not an agent of a person." Merit systems became increasingly accepted and increasingly extensive, gradually reaching their way up to the higher ranks of government. Napoleon in particular had insisted that even top level personnel should be recruited on the basis of ability. The French upper class, being the best educated, was still able to capture most of these positions. However, since only the most capable of the upper class received the favor of government appointment, social prestige was able to join forces with personal capacity to impart considerable luster to the position of senior public servant. The French civil service today still benefits from this development.

As the trend toward formalized, systematized, and depersonalized government continued, it produced a major theoretician. A brilliant German sociologist named Max Weber took a long look at what was happening and liked what he saw. He then proceeded to set down the hypotheses and the categories needed to understand, evaluate, and, if you will, promote this new phenomenon, a phenomenon which he called bureaucracy.

BUREAUCRACY TRIUMPHANT

Weber viewed administration as falling into one of three categories. The first type was based on the charismatic leader principle. This principle is a simple one. The man on top rules more or less absolutely and everything that the organization does is a product of, or is subject to, his particular will and whim. True, the leader may delegate duties and responsibility. He may even delegate substantial authority. But it is always the leader who makes the arrangements and decides the circumstances and woe to the delegatee who forgets this. The organization administered by the leader principle is the reflection, if not the embodiment, of one man's personality.

The second type of administration in Weber's classification was the traditional. Under this arrangement, administrative positions are established and assigned on the basis of custom. Who one is, not what one can do, determines just what one will do. This principle governed to a great extent the makeup of the German Army's officer corps in Weber's day and is still seen in operation in many underdeveloped countries. As a matter of fact, it has not yet vanished from the Deep South of the United States.

The third type of administration was bureaucratic. Here the posts are created and handed out on the basis of fixed principle and functional capabilities. Traditional custom and leader intervention play little role in the handling of specific cases. As a later writer, Professor Robert Dubin, has put it, "bureaucratic administration frees the organization from absolute rule by a single individual and from the dead hand of the past."

Weber firmly believed that the administrative mechanism which evolves from the precepts of bureaucracy compares with other administrative devices the same way that a machine compares with a non-mechanical method of production. The bureaucratic mechanism should further and foster such praiseworthy administrative qualities as continuity, discretion, unity, strict though impartial subordination, reduction of friction, reduction of material and personnel costs, and knowledge of the files.

Says sociologist Peter Blau in summing up the Weberian concept, "Its official nature . . . develops the more perfectly the more bureaucracy is 'dehumanized,' the more completely it succeeds in eliminating from official business love, hatred, and all purely personal, material and emotional elements which escape calculation." The word calculation plays a particularly important role in Weber's theory for he continually emphasized the dependency of bureaucratic mechanisms on "calculable rules."

The bureaucratic mechanism requires a systematic division of labor which, Weber pointed out, gives birth to specialization. The work is distributed to the subunits in an orderly and regular manner. Weber assumed "a consistent system of abstract rules . . . (and) the application of these rules to particular cases." Decisions in a bureaucracy are not made arbitrarily by whim or caprice or intuition but according to the "book."

The operation of an organization along such lines brings into being a hierarchical structure with each lower office subject to the authority of one above it. However, no higher office can tyrannize its subordinate; it can only hold the lower office responsible for carrying out its fixed allotment of duties. Similarly, no higher official can exercise tyrannical power over a subordinate. He can only hold him accountable for discharging his impersonal and official obligations.

The officials themselves are to be chosen on the basis of technical qualification, and these qualifications are to be judged by strictly objective standards. Once chosen, these officials will not enter or leave the system simply as a result of a change in leadership or political control. Their work will constitute a career and they will advance to higher posts through an impartial system. This system could be based on either seniority or performance or, as was most often the case, a combination of the two. Just what emphasis was given to what criteria did not matter as long as the criteria were fixed, neutral, and objective.

As developed by Weber, bureaucratic theory seemed a wholly rational response to the problems of the 20th century. Government activity was proliferating, engulfing government leaders with a flood tide of work and problems. Woodrow Wilson, writing at about the same time as Weber, pointed out that for the first time in history, "it is getting harder to run a constitution than it is to frame one." Smooth running bureaucratic machines seemed the answer. Weber himself felt that bureaucracy offered the only sensible way of organizing mass society. To him, modern government had only one basic choice: bureaucracy or dilettantism.

Bureaucracy thus came to be hailed as the triumph of rationality and its praises soon resounded from one end of the administrative spectrum to the other. And rationality was not the only garland draped around its neck. It drew enthusiastic plaudits as a crowning achievement in the growth of democracy as well. This may sound preposterous to many young people today but a little reflection may show that there is merit to the claim. Bureaucracy's key concept of impartiality embodied the key democratic concept of equality. Since it operated without discrimination or arbitrariness, treating both employees and clients without fear or favor, its emergence marked a giant step forward toward the achievement of a democratic system. It is not an accident that its growth paralleled the growth of a democratic political culture.

This can be seen vividly in what happened in Weber's native Germany after his death. The Weimar Republic, that earnest but woefully fragile experiment in German democracy, extended and strengthened bureaucratic norms and values throughout the country. Indeed, Weber was something of an idol to administrators during those days. The advent of Nazism, however, crushed much of this development. As Professor Frederick S. Burin has noted, "regularity, legality, formalism, neutrality and the objective, non-arbitrary application of calculable legal norms, regardless of content, to all persons and situations . . . were utterly incompatible with the Nazi spirit of charismatic leadership, ideological mysticism ('we think with our blood') and arbitrary decisionism. In theory and practice, the Nazis rejected calculable rules . . . in favor of discretionary measures geared in every instance with the exigencies of the moment."

Stalin's Russia also displayed little respect for bureaucratic concepts. Promotions and dismissals were often, perhaps usually, made arbitrarily. Stalin's son Vassily, so his sister Svetlana tells us in her memoirs, was promoted to the rank of lieutenant general in the Air Force at the age of 24 even though he was so drunk most of the time that he could not even climb aboard a plane, much less fly one. The abusive activities of the various Soviet police forces, and the dismissal and, in some cases, persecution of Jewish administrators in 1950, are other examples of nonbureaucratic behavior. It is interesting to note that the somewhat halting steps toward detyrannization which the USSR has taken since Stalin's death have led to greater use of such bureaucratic norms as specialization, promotion according to merit, etc.

In the industrial West, the United States lagged behind many other countries in climbing aboard the bureaucratic bandwagon. Americans chafe under formalized and systematized procedures and so we held out the longest in accepting bureaucracy as a way of governmental life. To some, this bears testament to our vigorous democratic spirit. Others, however, view it somewhat differently, feeling that our lack of affinity for bureaucratic norms and values reflect our disrespect for the standards of equal treatment and our relentless quest for favoritism and preference. In practice, Americans tend to join organizations, including semimilitary ones, faster than West Europeans, and public opinion polls show us to be much less tolerant of political, social, and sexual deviation than our fellow Westerners in the Old World. Thus our antibureaucratic leaning may not indicate a rejection of conformity but something quite different.

In any case, bureaucracy finally began to blossom on American soil during the 1930s. Spearheading its development were the liberal elements of the nation. Opposing its growth were the country's conservatives and reactionaries. For a while, bureaucrats assumed roles of near-heroes as they proceeded to battle big business and to ride roughshod over local elites and political bigwigs in order to extend the benefits of a welfare state to one and all. In 1948, Paul Appleby published a book entitled *Big Democracy* in which he pleaded an enthusiastic case for bureaucratic power. He lovingly dedicated the work to "Bill Bureaucrat" who he said was working for a better America. No reviewer found such a dedication at all strange.

BUREAUCRACY EMBATTLED

Despite its mushrooming growth during the 1930s and 1940s, bureaucracy never gained the sweep and acceptance in the United States that it did in most other developed countries. And when the tide began to turn against bureaucracy in the 1950s, the United States was the first to register the signs of discontent. There is an irony here for, in some respects, it was the lack of bureaucratic development in our organizational life which helped trigger the revolt against it. It is our state and local governments that have customarily delivered most of government's services to the citizenry and had these governments developed more formalized, systematized, and equitable methods of operation, the revolt might have been delayed. The same holds true of business as well. It was the growing tendency of corporations to check into their employees' political and social life and to make judgments based on criteria other than neutral competence which produced the first expressed signs of corporate malaise.

In any case, an antiorganization movement began to take shape in the United States during the 1950s. It usually lumped bureaucratic and nonbureaucratic organizations together but this came to matter less and less. Even those who could tell the difference were beginning to feel that none of the existing types of organizations could any longer meet the needs and demands of modern man.

One of the first to question our organizational life was the economist Kenneth E. Boulding. In 1953, he published *The Organizational Revolution* in which he viewed with concern if not alarm the growing role of organizations in modern society. Boulding claimed that such ethical values as freedom, justice, love, etc. tended to run at cross-purposes with, and thus lose out to, such organizational features as power, impersonality, etc.

Three years later, William H. Whyte's *The Organization Man* appeared on the bookstands. It was a slashing indictment of business organizations, documenting in abundant and colorful detail how such concerns were undermining the freedom and personality of their employees. It is interesting to note that Whyte himself was an editor of the nation's foremost business magazine *Fortune* and that his book evoked enthusiastic praise from many of the "establishment's" media including *The New York Times*.

A year later, Chris Argyris published *Personality and Organization* which sought to make a scholarly case for the essential conflict which Argyris claimed must exist between the needs of the individual and the needs of the organization. This conflict, he said, tended to feed on itself. Since the employees and the managers have divergent interests and goals, they tend to act in ways which only exacerbate the conflict between them. As a result, argued Argyris, an organization usually becomes transformed into a system of dynamic tension. Employees often set up informal organizations as a way of getting around or even sabotaging the formal organization which they often view as an enemy. According to Argyris, the employee has a thrust toward "self-actualization" which the organizational structure continually tends to thwart.

As the antiorganizational movement gained momentum in the 1960s, it began to center its attack more specifically on bureaucracy itself and its cherished ideals. It accused bureaucracy of fostering an emphasis on routinization. The knowledge of the files which Weber praised as a wholesome advancement in administration became, for a growing number of critics, an anathema. In a world of increasing complexity and challenge, it was deemed a waste and even a crime to squander attention on trivia. Then the formalized and systematized procedures of bureaucracy came under fire for promoting delay and inflexibility, qualities which were held unacceptable in a dynamic, technological society. The tendency to promote employees on the basis of longevity was also scored for failing to encourage them to make the fullest use of their capabilities and for allowing leadership often to pass into the hands of the less competent. Finally, even the most prized of the bureaucratic norms, neutral competence, found itself being weighed in the balance and found wanting. As the civil rights movement took hold of wider areas of American life, the feeling began to spread that objective tests and criteria were retarding minority group advancement. If a black principal with fewer degrees could administer a school with black children better than a white principal with more degrees, then neutral competence was now a bar rather than a spur to efficiency.

At the heart of many of these criticisms was a rejection of bureaucracy's core concept, depersonalization. The removal of personal whim and caprice from organizational life had once been a major target of those seeking to affirm and enhance human dignity. It had now ceased to be so. Depersonalization had become equated with dehumanization. The world had indeed moved on.

This mounting antipathy to bureaucratic culture did not confine itself to any particular sector or sectors of the political spectrum, but spread itself throughout the entire society. "The federal bureaucracy, whose growth and problems were once only the concern of the right, has now become a major concern of the left, the center and almost all points in between," wrote Professor James Q. Wilson in 1967. "Conservatives once feared that a powerful bureaucracy would work a social revolution. The left now fears that this same bureaucracy is working a conservative reaction. And the center fears that the bureaucracy isn't working at all."

So pervasive has the sentiment against bureaucracy become that it has now infected bureaucrats themselves. In 1968, Dwight Waldo, the grand old man of American public administration, set up a conference of younger men in the field to find out what they were thinking. The conference was held in Syracuse University's Minnowbrook Lodge and lasted three and a half days. The participants, all in their 20s and 30s, represented 27 universities and government agencies. Those who attended described it afterwards as a hectic, chaotic, but, at the same time, exhilarating affair which saw prepared conference papers discarded and lively, on-going and small group discussion substituted in their place. A consensus soon emerged that the old bureaucratic ideals had outlived their usefulness and that new structures and methods should take their place.

After the conference, two of its participants polled the general membership of the American Society for Public Administration to test their reaction to the various issues which the conference raised. The canvassers were surprised and delighted to learn that many of their concerns and discontents were shared by a majority of older practitioners in the field.

The rising distaste for traditional bureaucracy has also begun to take hold abroad. The Fulton Commission set up by the British Government in the mid-1960s to assess the British civil service came out with a majority report harshly critical of the way Britain's bureaucracy was operating. All four civil servants on the commission shared the majority point of view and signed the report. In Germany, the Social Democratic Party campaigned successfully in 1969 on a platform which called for ending "the strict bureaucratic hierarchical principle." In France where, somewhat like the United States, antibureaucratic sentiments have always been in vogue, the Gallic natives are showing signs of yet greater restlessness. Toward the end of the 1960s, French farmers had taken to dumping manure on the door steps of public officials while commuters with only second-class tickets had made forays en masse into first-class rail compartments. These and other events pointed to a swelling sense of outrage on the part of citizens against a government which had promulgated some 22,000 administrative regulations.

In Italy, public dissatisfaction with governmental operations forced the government to create a special ministry for the reform of the bureaucracy. One incident reported by the British writer Arthur Sampson may indicate why. During the early 1960s, says Sampson, "a mysterious intruder used to clamber into civil service offices, muddle up the files and reduce them to chaos, leaving behind a message signed 'enemy of bureaucracy.' He became a kind of national hero."

MAC GREGOR'S MANIFESTO

As problems arise, solutions emerge to meet them. As the organizational malaise was infecting wider areas of the social fabric, remedies began to appear. Argyris noted in his 1957 indictment that organizations don't have to function in an antihumanistic manner. He urged them to adopt more democratic leadership and give their employees enlarged roles and wider areas of responsibility. He felt that such steps would actually benefit organizations as well as the individuals who compose them. The conflict he postulated between the former and the latter does not *have* to exist.

The young men who met in Minnowbrook were of a similar view. They felt that organizations, at least those in the public sector, could become more flexible and responsive, both to those they employed and those they served. And the name they frequently cited to support their views was that of Douglas MacGregor.

A lanky, amiable, pipe smoking, professor from the Midwest, Douglas MacGregor hardly seems to have been type cast to play the role of revolutionary. But, as it turned out, this is what has happened.

Born in Detroit in 1906, MacGregor took his Ph.D. in psychology in Harvard in the mid-1930s and stayed on to spend two years teaching social psychology. He then went to M.I.T. and rose quite rapidly up the academic hierarchy from instructor to full professor. He was serving as executive director of M.I.T.'s Industrial Relations Section in 1948 when he left to become president of Antioch College. Six years later he returned to M.I.T., this time as a professor of industrial management. He also served as consultant to many larger corporations and government agencies before his untimely death in 1964. MacGregor thus had ample experience in both theory and practice, and, in terms of the latter alone, in both public, private, and semipublic institutions. He was consequently well-equipped to write the manifesto for the administrative revolution.

In his book *The Human Side of Enterprise* in 1960 and in many papers, articles, and addresses throughout his none-too-long life, MacGregor enunciated a philosophy designed to bring administration into its postbureaucratic phase. He took the work of Brandeis University psychologist Abraham Maslow as his starting point. Maslow had claimed that human needs were ordered into a hierarchy and that as a human being obtains satisfaction for one level of needs, he reaches up to the next. At the bottom of the ladder are physiological or physical needs. These are basic needs which must be met before attending to all others. Yet, they have little upward thrust. "Consider your need for air," said MacGregor in discussing this theory. "Except as you are deprived of it, it has no motivating effect on your behavior." And he added, "man lives by bread alone only when there is no bread."

After his physical needs are satisfied, man shifts his attention to safety needs. Now he wants security from danger and deprivation of every kind. Once these needs are taken care of, he begins to focus attention on his social needs. Fellowship, warmth, human contact, and beneficent interaction leap to the forefront of his interest calendar. Then, as soon as these social needs are assuaged, man's ego needs come into play. At this juncture, he seeks to improve his esteem in the eyes of his fellows and himself through acquiring competence and registering achievement.

The satisfaction of ego needs prepares him for ascending to the highest plateau of the needs ladder, the need for self-fulfillment. At this level, man's drive centers on the development of his potentialities and the utilization of his creativity in the fullest sense of the word.

MacGregor accused organizational management of failing to recognize that satisfied needs were not an impetus to behavior. Once certain needs are met, other needs must be answered. "Management by direction and control—whether implemented with the hard, the soft or the firm-but-fair approach—fails under today's conditions to provide effective motivation toward organizational objectives," he wrote. "It fails because direction and control are useless methods of motivating people whose physiological and safety needs are reasonably satisfied and whose social, egoistic and self-fulfillment needs are predominant."

MacGregor continually emphasized that organizations could not meet their modern day challenges by simply acting charitably toward their employees. The problem was much greater than that. "People in general do not give their loyalties or their efforts out of gratitude; in fact it makes them feel a little uncomfortable to be put into a dependent position. We have had several instances across the country of severe strikes and violent upheavals in companies that have been noted for their excessive paternalism. Employees who, to all intents and purposes have everything, stand up in rebellion and say 'we don't want to be given things.' Behind that is a certain feeling, perhaps, that it lowers their sense of importance to have somebody else decide what is good for them."

If neither the "be good" nor "be tough" policy would any longer accomplish the job, then what would? MacGregor summed up his answer in one word: self-direction. "In the recognition of human beings to exercise self-control lies the only fruitful opportunity for industrial management to realize the full potential represented by professional resources," he said.

MacGregor's use of the term "professional resources" merits special attention. He felt that the growing utilization of professional people in industry, as well as in other kinds of organizations, gave particular thrust and urgency to his theory. We will have more to say about this important trend later on. Suffice it for the moment to note that, in Mac-Gregor's view, such developments as the explosive growth of science, the rapidly increasing complexity of technology in both office and factory, the growing complexity of industry-society relations, and the growing "white collarization" of the work force were making such self-direction not only desirable but necessary.

MacGregor called his new approach Theory Y and contrasted it to traditional and more authoritarian managerial methods which he termed Theory X. His Theory Y encompassed many new and unorthodox techniques. These included increased decentralization of power and delegation of responsibility, enlargement of the scope of most jobs, employee participation and consultative management, and performance appraisals in which the employee himself does most of the appraising. We will be exploring such concepts and their application in depth and detail in subsequent chapters.

Does all this mean complete abandonment by management of its prerogatives? Is all control to be surrendered? Not really. MacGregor borrowed a concept from Peter Drucker to replace the control devices used in authoritarian Theory X organizations. This new concept is called management by objectives. It requires managers to set certain objectives and then simply hold the employee responsible for fulfilling them without exercising hour-by-hour or even day-by-day supervision. However, Theory Y does not even allow managers full rights in this area for MacGregor urged that the employees be allowed to set up their own objectives with the advice and approval of their superiors.

In pleading his case to management, MacGregor pointed out that the Theory Y method enabled them to offer employees those benefits which management not only had in abundance but also which, if given to employees, would not leave management poorer but richer. These benefits were prestige, knowledge, and a sense of achievement. "The supply of such opportunities—unlike the supply of money—is unlimited," said MacGregor.

"The ingenuity and the perseverance of industrial management in the pursuit of economic ends have changed many scientific and technological dreams into commonplace realities," he wrote. "It is now becoming clear that the application of the same talents to the human side of enterprise will not only enhance substantially these materialistic achievements but will bring us one step closer to the 'good society.'

"Shall we get on with the job?"

2

THE CRUMBLING PYRAMID

Wherever two or three people gather together, one among them is likely to wield some authority over the others. Such authority may be only informal. It may also be quite limited in extent. And it may even be only temporary. But it is likely to exist since all organizations, including the loosest and most voluntary ones, have found that some have to assume more responsibility than others. Responsibility has never been deemed useful without authority commensurate with its effective discharge. Thus hierarchy has been the oldest, the most persistent and, to many, the most annoying aspect of human organization.

The arrival of bureaucracy on the administrative scene brought some changes in this aspect of human organization. First, the exercise of authority was restricted. As we have seen, the members and subalterns in a bureaucratic organization can only be held accountable for their official duties and for dischargining them in the prescribed ways. Second, the organization itself became a developed and compartmentalized structure with each member and subunit having its well-defined place.

To meet these requirements, the bureaucratic organization inevitably takes a form resembling an isosceles triangle. Those at the bottom form the broad base; those in the middle levels gradually diminish in number; at the apex, one person bears the ultimate responsibility. The well-wrought pyramid stands as the symbol, the coat of arms, of modern bureaucracy.

Within the pyramid, work goes on. Authority starts at the top and filters down through the organization, thinning out as it spreads itself over wider and wider areas. Communication flows upward, converging at the apex. By such devices as an orderly chain of command, which keeps these currents running up and down, and a reasonable span of control, so that no middle manager has too few or too many subunits under him, the organization's activity is supposed to run smoothly.

The model which most clearly exemplifies this arrangement is the infantry division. The rank and file are formed into squads led by sergeants; the squads form platoons headed by lieutenants; the platoons form companies under the command of captains, and so on up to the commanding general. All pertinent pieces of information arising from the subunits reach their resting place in his office, while it is from his office that the overall direction of the division emerges. The organizational chart of an infantry division displays a geometric neatness which makes it seem a triumph of administrative development.

However, like so many of man's synthetic constructs, organizational schemes are one thing on paper and another thing in reality. Authority is supposed to flow downward in smooth, consistent currents in a bureaucratic organization, but is this always the case? Not usually. Often it gets dammed up at one point and tends to spill over too generously into another. Sometimes it even seems to reverse course as a key figure at a lower level manages to exercise considerable control over his ostensible superior. Many a top sergeant has bent his lieutenant or even his captain to his will and whim. Communication meanwhile often has an even rougher course making its way to the top. There is always too much material to be communicated and so some selectivity and distortion tends to enter into the filtering process as it journeys to the apex. There is a distinct tendency, also, for a lower unit to pass up information that it thinks the higher units want to have, but to suppress or change information which does not meet this standard. Furthermore, information that reaches the top is likely to be somewhat outdated by the time it gets there. This means those who make the most sweeping and crucial decisions must act on information that is likely to be less reliable and less fresh than that which is available to their subunits.

Our modern technological society is generating changes which intensify these organizational problems considerably. So many people at the lower levels are now doing so many different and complicated things that it is becoming increasingly difficult for those at the higher levels to know just what is going on. And even when they know and understand what is going on, they still have difficulty exercising control since those presumed to be under them may have motivations and loyalties which do not yield so easily to the normal exercise of bureaucratic authority.

This brings us to another problem, that of the staff specialist. Modern administrative theory usually distinguishes two basic categories of personnel—line and staff. The line personnel are those charged with directly fulfilling the organization's purposes. In a fire department they fight the fires; in a school department, they teach the children; in a canning factory, they manufacture and distribute the cans. The staff personnel are supposed to assist the line people. Staff employees run the computers, draw up the personnel procedures, repair the equipment, etc.

As soon as the first staff person makes his entry on the organizational stage, he disrupts the tableau. There is no place for him in the organizational subunits which fit so snugly into the compact organizational triangle. As soon as the staff specialist appears, the pyramid starts to develop unseemly bulges and sagging lines.

If we take a large modern high school in a metropolitan community as an example, we will find the line personnel, namely the teachers, responsible to department chairmen who are, in turn, responsible to the principal. The addition of janitors and secretaries complicates but does not fundamentally alter the triangular distribution of authority. However, when we add the guidance counselor, the school psychologist or social worker, the data processing expert, and others, we immediately start to rock the bureaucratic boat. Such people cannot be placed into the regular line departments. Furthermore, although they may not be more extensively trained and may not receive any greater salary than the teachers, their relationship with the department chairmen and the principal is quite different. Frequently, for example, a school social worker with a master's degree will be working in close and frequent contact with the principal while a teacher with a comparable degree will enjoy no such direct relationship. Finally, while the school social worker is usually under the general jurisdiction of the principal, she may also be more directly responsible to a special services director who has his seat of power in the superintendent's office. Thus the control which the principal, let alone the department chairmen, may exercise over her is often limited.

The social worker is also not primarily an educator, and this further disrupts the authority structure. Trained in, and committed to, a different profession than the educators, she has her own way of viewing problems and her own way of approaching them. And since she has her own specialized expertise, the line personnel, including the principal, often have difficulty in making any but the most basic judgements as to how well she is discharging her duties.

The use of such specialists in modern high schools is increasing. The social worker, the guidance counselor, and the data processing expert are of fairly recent vintage. Their ranks are growing as visual aides, in-service training, and other modern developments become an increasing part of the high school's operations. Even the line personnel themselves are taking on the coloration and creating some of the problems of staff employees as they themselves become more specialized. The teacher of the school's retarded children, for example, may have specialized training along with individual motivations and goals which may well set her somewhat apart from the rest of the teachers. And, like the social worker, she may be less accountable to the school principal than to a director of special education who is situated in the school system's downtown headquarters.

The growing use of staff specialists and the growing specialization of line personnel is thus playing havoc with bureaucratic organizations. Authority is becoming ever more diminished and confused. Not only are those above having an increasingly difficult time keeping abreast of, let alone controlling, those below but, in a very real sense, it is becoming harder and harder to tell just who is below and who is above. The brilliant specialist often outshines his more pedestrian supervisor. We all know, for instance, that Christian Barnard made the first success-ful heart transplant; how many of us know who is the head of the South African hospital in which he works? It is hard to peg the specialist in a status ladder and it may be impossible to arrange a group of special-ists into a hierarchical order for each may not only be as skilled but also as indispensable as the other. As Peter Drucker has pointed out "knowledge work knowns no hierarchy for there are no 'higher' and no 'lower' knowledges." Every knowledge worker is, in some respects, an executive. As the number of knowledge workers in virtually all organi-zations continues to grow—they are expected to make up half of the work force by the end of the 1970s—hierarchical structures tend to collapse. Pyramids become increasingly dysfunctional as organizations find themselves with more and more chiefs and fewer and fewer Indians.

But if the exercise of managerial control is becoming ever more dif-ficult, it is also becoming ever less necessary. "It is part of the professional unique value," MacGregor once noted, "that he is capable of determining the steps necessary to achieve the desired objective." Professor Dale E. Zand goes even further. "It doesn't make sense to insist that a man should produce twice as many bright ideas in two hours as he produces in one hour," notes Zand. And he adds, "Traditional methods of supervision emphasize regularity, measurement of work in process and orderly appearance. When this form of supervision is rigidly enforced in the knowledge organization it may not only be ineffective but actually obstructive." A mounting pile of evidence supports such concerns. For example, in a study of 14 municipal health departments, Dennis J. Palumbo found that centralization and formalization, two of bureaucracy's cornerstones, were *inversely* related to professionalization. In other words, as professionalism went up, bureaucratization went down.

The stepped-up use of staff personnel and the growing professionalization and specialization of line personnel is also aiding and abetting another trend which undermines the bureaucratic pyramid. This trend is the increased rate of change. According to the National Commission of Technology, Automation and Economic Progress, it took about 30 years to make a technical discovery commercially applicable in the pre-World War I era. Between the wars, the time span fell to 16 years. After World War II, the gap between discovery and wholesale application narrowed to nine years, and appears to be decreasing all the time. In 1966, an executive of Fairchild Camera pointed out that half of the products which the firm expected to be making in five years did not then even exist.

All of this imposes great strains on the bureaucratic way of doing things. Traditional line personnel and their managers usually become well-enmeshed in the organizational fabric and often resist change unless it involves increments of salary, time off, etc. More professionalized line people, however, usually have a greater commitment to a body of knowledge and a system of techniques. They customarily have some interest in improving the conditions that will allow this knowledge and these techniques to be more effectively utilized. As for staff specialists, they have still less investment in the organizational structure since they are rarely an integral part of it. In many cases, they do not even spend all their working time within it. Far from hindering change, they are often eager to see the organization's structure altered to facilitate the play of their own skills and the fulfillment of their own goals. The explosive growth of knowledge which modern society is undergoing is creating more specialization as it creates change. And this specialization is, in turn, accelerating the process of change. The knowledge revolution thus fosters and feeds the administrative revolution.

Change means that those in leadership roles today may have to yield such positions to those with different skills tomorrow. Change means that communication must not only flow upward through the organization but also flow horizontally through it. Change means that rules and regulations, one of bureaucracy's most sacrosanct features, must wither and shrink. As Anthony Downs points out, "Rules and regulations are most efficacious when the organization is carrying out routine and repetitive tasks. The more unpredictable and variable are the situations faced by a bureaucracy in carrying out its functions, the less likely it is to be governed by such rules." Thus the age of innovation is sweeping up more and more organizations in a flood tide of progress. As an employee of a California public agency which was adapting to a new situation once said, "What we need is an organization chart put together like an airline schedule, subject to change without notice."

Such developments as professionalization, specialization, and innovation are thus spelling doom for the bureaucratic mystique. Its structure can no longer cope with the society in which it seeks to function. The structure of the modern organization may show less similarity to the Egyptian pyramids than it does to the shifting sands around them.

FROM TRIANGLE TO CIRCLE

To replace the crumbling pyramid, a new organizational structure is emerging. I say emerging, not emerged, for what took thousands of years to evolve will not vanish in a night or a year. However, the contours of this new structure are already beginning to appear. A rough-hewn model is now available and, as we shall see, many functioning organizations have already successfully adopted at least some of its features. More are doing so all the time.

The new organizational form does not display the smooth compactness of the bureaucratic pyramid. As might be expected, this post-bureaucratic paradigm is a loose, amorphous, and sprawling affair. Furthermore, it is constantly changing. It is perhaps best visualized as a squishy, uneven circle within which clusters of small units, like amoeba, constantly form and reform. At the center there is a more or less stationary cluster which is connected by lines to all the others. However, the center cluster, while it may more or less stay in the same general position within the circle, also undergoes changes in shape from time to time. Furthermore, there is no single unit at the exact center of even this center cluster, and the lines that come into this central cluster from all the others do not all terminate at the same point but at various units within it.

If we look at all these lines a little more closely, we notice two other distinctive features. First, there are not only lines connecting the floating clusters with the center one, but there are also many lines connecting these clusters with one another. Secondly, these lines, whether they connect floating clusters with the central one or with one another, are never pulled taut. They show considerable slackness, thus enabling the floating clusters to move around pretty much as they please.

When we translate this model into a word picture we see an organization consisting of small groups engaged in specific tasks. For the most part, these task forces are made up of staff specialists and professional line personnel. The staffers often outnumber the liners in these clusters and, in any case, it is difficult to tell one from the other. As the task on which any group is working is completed, the task force dissolves with its members joining new groups that are constantly forming. The center cluster consists of management along with various support services which the task forces utilize as they feel the need. But management is now multiheaded, hence there is no subunit in the exact center.

Cross-communication has become a vital element in the new circular or globular organization. This accounts for all the lines connecting the various clusters. However, the fact that there are lines joining each cluster with some point in the circle's nucleus shows that there is some degree of managerial control. The center can still rein in any group which is floating too far afield or getting in another group's way. But, on a day-to-day basis, management's function is more one of coordination and support rather than the exercise of authority.

Such is the basic model of the new nonpyramidal organization. To what extent does it reflect reality? To what extent does it describe organizations already in existence?

No organization ever fully lives up to any model which may be drawn to depict it. The circular organizational model just described fits no existing organization at this time and will probably not com-

pletely portray any organization that is likely to come into existence
in the foreseeable future. Yet, it suggests the contours of several highly
successful organizations which exist today. Since these organizations
offer suggestions regarding the efficacy and direction of the administrative revolution, we will now briefly examine four of them. Two are in
the public sector, two are in the private sector, and all four provide
examples of the nature of administration in the postbureaucratic age.

THEORY Y AT WORK: THE ISRAELI ARMY,
THE CALIFORNIA STATE INSURANCE COMPENSATION FUND

In 1956, the tiny army of Irael put to almost instant rout an opposing
Egyptian force that was several times larger, much better equipped,
and geographically far better positioned. Air power was not as decisive
a factor in this affray as it was to be in the second confrontation in
1967. The first battle of the Sinai was essentially a land war and the
encounter was decided in the field. The speed and manner in which
it was decided provoked immediate interest in the organization which
carried it off.

A retired Brigadier General of the United States Army, S.L.A. Marshall, journeyed to Israel after the 1957 action to determine for himself
what happened. In an article in *Harper's* magazine, he reported what he
had found. And as a career military man, what he had found somewhat
startled him.

General Marshall discovered the Israeli victory to be even more impressive than he had originally surmised. The Israeli forces had to
advance over an area that was not only heavily fortified but also topo-
graphically difficult. The Egyptian troops held the high ground and
the Israelis had to proceed against a flat field of fire. Furthermore,
Marshall discovered that many of the Egyptian units fought bravely.
Yet, the attacking Israelis managed to advance with alacrity and comparative ease. "Hitting forces traveled farther over more formidable
country in less time than any other combat body," he noted.

Marshall also came across another aspect of the war which, as a
military man, he found yet more jolting. It was when enemy pressure
was at its maximum and when "disorganization should have ensued"
that the Israeli Army reached its maximum efficiency.

What was responsible for such an amazing military performance?

The first thing which piqued Marshall's military curiosity was the Israeli Army's heavy, and, for a military organization, unusual emphasis on what we might call Theory Y values. Men are treated and taught to treat others humanely. On training marches, for example, recruits who fall out from exhaustion are carried by their comrades. Such incidents seldom occur, however, because the men are rested at every opportunity instead of being subjected to maximum strain. " 'Don't be too eager; don't pile on the pressure' has an odd sound coming from a General Staff," observed the former American general but he found this to be the standard operating policy in the army he was studying.

As an example, Marshall cited a frequent custom in other military forces. The colonel tells his captains to be ready at 0900. The captains tell their platoon leaders to be ready at 0800. And the platoon leaders, in turn, tell their squad leaders to be ready at 0700. "Israel's army shuns this practice like the plague," reported Marshall. "The recruit on his way to become an NCO is told that if he checks his men and they look relatively ready, even if they are still sleeping, then it is a sign of weakness in him if he routs them out ten minutes too early to further his own peace of mind."

Facilitating the observance of such norms is the Israeli system of officer training. All officers are chosen from the ranks and each must serve at least six months as a private and six months as an NCO before being commissioned. Little emphasis, meanwhile, is placed on age. Thus, the average age of an Israeli lieutenant on being commissioned is 19. The teen-aged officer would be immediately put in command of soldiers who might be two and a half times older.

Given such factors as these, hierarchy, as might be expected, plays a greatly reduced role in the Israeli Army. Saluting, the traditional military symbol of deference to authority, is causual. Privates often address officers by their first names and sometimes by their nicknames. Dress and even discipline is also casual. An officer was seen wearing striped civilian socks with his military uniform; a sentry was noticed muching an orange as he marched his post. Yet despite all these signs of what would seem to be organizational slackness, Marshall found an extremely high degree of coordination. Cross-communication flourished and intra-organizational rivalries were at a minimum. He attributed this to the nonbureaucratic, personalized nature of the system. As one staff officer told him, "We give and take more easily because we are all friends."

How, then, does management manage in such a loose system? Apparently by objectives. "All that counts is the end object which discipline elsewhere is supposed to serve . . ." The army's entire approach resembled, at least to some extent, task force operations in the circular organizational model we have examined. Leaders of small units are trained and encouraged to make their own decisions as to how to perform their tasks and they were to be continually prepared for sudden changes in conditions. The high command, meanwhile, constantly stressed the need for leadership rather than direction. "Success comes when leaders lead instead of push," Marshall was told.

There are many other aspects of the administrative revolution which are found in the Israeli Army and we will discuss some of these later. For the present, suffice it to note that at a time when discontent with Theory X organizational systems was starting to brew in Europe and the United States, an organization of a type which traditionally has been most Theory X oriented, namely an army, had already tried out a good deal of the Theory Y approach. And had found that it worked.

Turning to this country and moving ahead a decade, we find a public organization in California offering a much more complete and illustrative, if less colorful, example, of how Theory Y principles can be put to use in the public sector. This is the California State Compensation Fund.

The Fund was organized in 1913 as an integral part of what was then a revolutionary concept of compulsory workmen's compensation, without regard to negligence or fault. The Fund was given the right and the encouragement to compete freely for the workmen's compensation insurance of private firms and to insure all public agencies unless they chose to assume their own liability. Functioning as a semi-independent public agency, the Fund grew and prospered.

However, by the mid-1960s it was starting to experience problems. For one thing, some California cities and counties which had been longtime customers of the fund began to insure themselves. For another, many private firms which had once given the fund their compensation insurance business had been taken over by conglomerate firms whose headquarters were located in other states. The insurance business of these former California companies was thus diverted to the out-of-state firms with whom their new parent companies had already been doing business. Consequently, while the Fund's insurance business was still growing, it was doing so at a declining rate. At the same time, its share of the market was going down.

This situation, added to the fact that internal strains and stresses brought on by the rapid population and industrial growth of California had also begun to make themselves increasingly felt, prompted the Fund's new manager, R. A. Young, to cast about for some new ways of operating. After exploring the subject with Neely Gardner, a management consultant and former State Training Officer, Young in 1967 decided to undertake an ambitious experiment in Theory Y.

One of the Fund's 24 district field offices was removed from the Fund's involved and cumbersome organizational structure and allowed to function pretty much on its own. Two of the 23 offices remaining within the organizational matrix were set up as control units or reference points. One of these offices was told of its role; the other was not.

As might be expected, the launching of such an experiment generated considerable tension and concern among the many sections of what had become a rather staid and highly bureaucratic agency. The first district manager of the experimental field office resigned. His replacement, however, fared much better. One of the new district manager's first steps was to set up a committee consisting of four staff members selected by their fellow employees. This committee was to plan the field office's future course. Shortly thereafter, special committees arose to explore special aspects of the office's new situation. To facilitate their work, the committee members were sent to a three-day training laboratory. This helped to break down hierarchical distinctions and bring out the interpersonal conflicts which had been hampering their work.

The planning committee and the special committees eventually developed a new structural pattern for the district office. Following intensive discussion by the entire staff, the plan was adopted and put into effect. The district office, cut adrift from its parent body, was now ready to sail pretty much under its own power and chart pretty much its own course. Its voyage toward some of administration's newer horizons did not prove to be consistently clear sailing; however, as it turned out, even some of the problems which developed had a positive aspect. For example, office turnover during the first year and a half of operation reached 30 percent. But according to an academic researcher who closely studied the experiment, all except one of these dropouts were people who, as a result of the experiment, felt they had finally discovered what they really wanted to do with their lives and it was this which prompted them to leave. The experiment was judged to be, for the most part, a great success and out of it emerged a whole new operational pattern for the California State Compensation Fund.

The new system which evolved from this experiment called for removing all district offices from the hierarchical structure which had encumbered and, to some extent, throttled them. They were now to receive their annual appropriations in a lump sum from the head office and decide for themselves how it was to be spent. The head office was to provide certain support services in the data processing, medical, and accounting areas but it was to be up to each district office to decide whether or not to utilize them. If it did, it would have to pay for them out of its appropriation. This not only encouraged the district offices to shop around for the best price but also encouraged these centralized service units to cut their costs and improve their efficiency. (They would, however, have an edge over private competitors since they were especially geared to provide services tailored to specific needs of the field units.)

In addition to offering specialized services, the Fund's central office exercises overall direction. However, management is by objectives. Each district office was to keep an acceptable set of records and to develop a program statement along with an economic blueprint for implementing it. What counted was performance as reflected in each field office's annual balance sheet.

Such a system of operations has allowed the Fund to abolish many hierarchical levels. Previously, the district managers would work under division managers and regional managers. Now they meet every month with the general manager. These monthly get-togethers are designed for the exchange of information and ideas and for the discussion of problems on a collegial basis.

The new system not only enables the district managers to meet directly with the general manager but also provides a similar opportunity to the rank and file.

A Program Advisory Council has been created consisting of two representatives elected from each field office. This council also meets regularly with the general manager to put forth ideas and suggestions. In order to make sure that as many points of view as possible are heard at these meetings and in order to enable as many employees as possible to participate in such decision-making activity, no employee is allowed to serve as his office's representative for more than one year. As the result of such procedures as these, decisions now tend to emerge from the units where the work is done and from the people who perform it.

What has happened to the old division chiefs and regional managers?

They now individually head program groups working on specific problems or they work on special assignments for the general manager. Generally, they have not felt unduly injured by this dehierarchization. In some important respects, they have experienced it as a benefit. Liberated from custodial-managerial duties and all the paper work such duties involve, they have found new challenges and new rewards in working on policy issues.

The experimental office itself, meanwhile, has gone forward with still more innovations. It was formerly divided, as were all the other field offices, into four sections on the basis of function. These were claims/rehabilitation, safety, sales, and auditing. It has replaced this grouping with work teams which amalgamate all four of these functions. The work teams themselves are created on the basis of clients served. As a result, a client now needs only to call one unit to obtain assistance on all four areas of Fund activity. This not only simplifies the client's task in securing the Fund's services but also makes certain that he is not given conflicting advice.

The California State Compensation Fund has thus put the "new administration" to the test with favorable and probably portentous results. Two background factors may have helped enable it to play such a trail-blazing role: the Fund is situated in a state whose governmental climate is well-disposed toward innovation, and it was originally set up to operate in a semi-independent fashion. The absence of such factors has curtailed the ability of most other government agencies to debureaucratize themselves. Consequently, it is the private sector which is moving further and faster toward administration's new frontiers. It is to this sector that we will now turn.*

THEORY Y AT WORK: NON-LINEAR SYSTEMS
AND ARTHUR D. LITTLE

In the early 1960s, a California-based manufacturing firm of technical equipment named Non-Linear Systems Incorporated took a long look at Theory Y and decided to swallow it whole. Or at least to swallow

* As this book was being finished, I received word from manager Young that the Fund no longer viewed their effort as an experiment. All the field offices were operating in this new fashion and the organizational change was now, in Young's words, "a fact of life."

as much of it as they could. They forthwith abolished their time clocks, their assembly line, and their pyramidal structure. In their place, they substituted a whole new system of industrial production.

To replace the assembly line, the company set up seven-man work teams, each of which was to build complete instruments. While each of these work groups was to be headed by an assistant assembly manager, all the members of each group were to join in deciding just what the group was to do and in what sequence it was to do it. In some cases, work groups were even allowed to write their own checks.

To coordinate this loosely-formed organizational structure and to formulate basic strategy and initiate action, Non-Linear Systems established an eight-member executive council. Each council member was to handle one goal-oriented work area such as market standing, innovation, profitability, productivity, physical and financial resources, worker attitude, performance, and public responsibility. Note that each work area was devised so that it did not place any one team exclusively under any one council member. Thus department managers at the firm often find themselves going to different council members as different problems arise. Often they will discuss a problem with two or three council members. The company president serves only as chairman of the council and assumes responsibility for one of the eight work areas.

Management at Non-Linear Systems soon came to be regarded as essentially an educational process and work in the company came to be more and more an educational experience. Classes were frequently held and members were encouraged to teach each other on the job. Employees were also encouraged to transfer frequently to various sections of the organization in order to improve their skills and broaden their general vocational and social experience.

The new setup not only fostered cross-communication but also markedly increased oral, as opposed to written, communication. Bureaucratic institutions usually thrive on written communication for it is supposed to promote preciseness and objectivity in thought and provide a record for the hallowed files as well. Written communication also saves the superior's time—he can read memos from five underlings in the time it takes to talk with one of them—and it protects the subordinate from accusations of error. However, as one of Non-Linear Systems' officers, Arthur Kuriloff, put it, "We believe that where there is mutual trust there is no need for protective paper," and so the company encouraged its employees to "say it, don't write it."

The switch to oral communication allowed the communicators to give emphasis through the use of gesture, tone, etc., to make sure that their message was received and to obtain an immediate feedback. While it did lead to greater subjectivity in decision-making, the company welcomed rather than feared such a development. "We have come to rely heavily on insight and feeling," Kuriloff noted some years after the new system was put into effect.

How has Non-Linear Systems fared with its Theory Y structure? In general, quite well. The system has worked most effectively at lower levels. The majority of the factory's employees are women, many of them housewives working to supplement the family income. They are not, therefore, a group in which one would expect to find a high degree of job commitment. But soon after Theory Y was inaugurated, a substantial number of these employees began taking courses in electronic theory outside of working hours.

What problems did emerge came at the highest level. It was the vice-presidents who were not yet ready for such a step and who had a hard time functioning without the support of whole departments under them. However, at last report, this problem was in the process of being resolved. Despite new competition, the company's work force, revenues, and profits show a significant rise over its former, more conventional days. Theory Y is alive and well in Del Mar, California.

At the other end of the country, meanwhile, a yet more extensive application of Theory Y is in full bloom. In Cambridge, Massachusetts, the 1600 employees of Arthur D. Little are busy working in an organizational structure which, in terms of the established precepts of administration, makes no sense whatsoever.

Arthur D. Little, Incorporated (ADL) was founded in 1886 as a chemical research company but has since diversified into nearly all fields of applied technology and economics. It is involved in developing various products and programs on its own and evaluating the products and programs of others. As a result of the nature of its work and the breadth of its activity, the company has developed an organizational structure that is so untraditional that it might not be called a structure at all. Indeed, the company has felt constrained to give prospective employees a seven-page statement outlining how it operates so that these applicants will know just what they are getting into. In terms of standard administrative behavior and organizational theory, the statement makes interesting reading.

"How does ADL work?," the statement asks. "First we should define our purpose and objectives. But this leads into difficulty; there is no single set of objectives that all professional staff members would agree upon as an adequate statement. Certainly, management has never made a formal statement of corporate objectives."

This does not mean that management has not been concerned with long-range planning. "Management has, however, often challenged the professional staff to consider what course of action it deems appropriate for the future of the business; the staff has responded vocally and actively and has in many instances put its own thinking into effect without stopping to wonder whether the actions met with management approval."

How does ADL react to such action? The statement itself is somewhat evasive, perhaps purposely so. It certainly gives no indication of disapproval and it makes a point of noting that management does not intend to state formal objectives of its own and also that it does not wish to interfere with the staff unnecessarily.

The basic organizational unit in ADL, as might be expected, is the work team which is built around a specific case or assignment. "The case leader need not be a designated member of the organizational hierarchy. Members of a case team are often more senior in areas of experience and/or higher in the administrative organization than the case (team) leader; but for the purposes of that case, they are expected to, and do, subordinate themselves to the technical and administrative direction of the case leader."

What is the role of top management in such an operation? "At ADL," continues the statement, "most high-ranking administrators consider their roles to be that of facilitating the work of the professional staff by providing staff services that relieve the professional of responsibility for such activities as detailed record-keeping, facilities, planning personnel search, and preliminary screening and coordination of salary information and actions." When it comes to exercising control, "they are also concerned about the maintaining of the work's highest professional standards, but these concerns do not manifest themselves in the form of interference with case leaders or attempts to manipulate them through the use of supervisors."

Group leaders do their own recruiting and their own evaluation of salaries, working in consultation with the personnel staff. When it comes to setting the salary of a new employee, ADL tends to pay the new employee what he himself thinks he's worth. He is then expected to demonstrate that he is worth his price. If he fails to do so, however, he is rarely fired although his employment status may undergo a change. Actually, a more frequent cause of separation from the company relates to the need for direction. Employees who are accustomed to functioning in a rather authoritarian structure and who may have certain dependency needs often find little satisfaction at ADL and eventually move on. The company recognizes this. It is the main reason why it gives prospective employees such a statement about its operations. Its function is to serve as a warning.

Some administrative structure, of course, does exist at ADL. The company is divided into five divisions, namely, Research and Development, Life Science, Engineering, Management Services, and what is called Division 500. Each division has a vice-president and a few senior employees within the division may report to him. However, these are usually highly competent professionals who simply do not wish to assume responsibility for managing a group. Essentially, the firm operates in an unstructured manner. The offices are open 24 hours a day and employees come and go pretty much as they wish. ADL proudly stresses that it has never issued an organization chart and never intends to do so.

Arthur D. Little has been a phenomenally successful business enterprise. Its work force increased 400 percent from the early 1950s to the late 1960s. At last report, it was still growing and prospering.

This brief look at Arthur D. Little and the other organizations provides a rough sketch of how Theory Y, or at least some of its features, operates. However, there are many other aspects of the new administration, and in the following chapters we will examine these in greater detail. These new patterns of administrative behavior point not only to a new form of organizational life but to a new society as well.

3

THE NEW CONVERGENCE

World War II left the nations of Western Europe exhausted and nearly prostrate. Those sectors of their economies which were not destroyed had become depreciated and run down. France's industrial capacity on V-E Day was only 40 percent of what it had been in 1938 —and 1938 was a depression year. Great Britain's position was scarcely much better while West Germany's situation was worse.

Housing and public facilities generally were also in a state of near shambles. France had lost nearly two million dwellings during the war. Other nations had sustained even greater depletions of housing supply. The bloody fighting which brought the war to its end had also wiped out bridges, schools, hospitals, water lines, and other vital facilities. Those that had been spared were badly deteriorated.

Finally, the war had also ravaged the continent's work force. Many of its most productive members had lost their lives. Others had become wholly or partly incapacitated. And most of the rest were physically and mentally exhausted. Thus, when the lights finally went on again in Western Europe, they revealed a grim and foreboding vista.

But bleak as the picture was, Western Europe's problems did not stop there. One hundred years before, Karl Marx had warned these countries of the specter of Communism. Now that specter was haunting them as never before. The disgust of their peoples with the performance of capitalism before the war, and the success of the Russian armies and the communist-lead resistance groups during the war, had provided fertile soil for sowing the seeds of discontent. Consequently, political parties dedicated, in whole or in part, to Marxist principles were in the ascendant. Whether they would triumph or not remained undetermined, but one thing was clear: the people of Western Europe would not be satisfied with a return to prewar conditions. They insisted on something better, much better.

The nations of Western Europe thus found themselves faced with two urgent challenges which seemed impossibly contradictory. They had to rebuild their shattered economies while at the same time they had to distribute more to their citizens. Put in other terms, they found themselves compelled both to save (invest resources in economic plant) and to spend (expend resources by increasing the pattern of welfare benefits).

To many, indeed to most, this looked like a baffling task. Even with the substantial American aid that was soon to be forthcoming, it would still be necessary to establish rigid priorities and abide by them. After all, one cannot spend the same money twice. If resources were to be invested in economic reconstruction, they could not be consumed through broadening and raising the level of social welfare. Even the British left-wing Labor leader Aneurin Bevan was willing to concede as much. Bevan once noted that if the British people had enjoyed full voting suffrage through the 19th century, Britain would never have undergone a successful industrial revolution. The people, acting through their elected representatives, would have eaten up all the surplus production, leaving little or nothing to carry out the painful process of industrial growth. Now, as Britain and the other war-scarred nations of Europe entered the postwar era, they faced the need for undergoing a second industrial revolution while simultaneously improving living standards and extending benefits. Their situation had all the appearances of a hopeless dilemma.

Fortunately, almost miraculously, appearances proved deceiving. When these war-weary nations set to work, the impossible happened. Welfare programs, instead of interfering with economic growth, actually seemed to encourage it. Economic capacities grew and living standards marched upward along with them. By the mid-1950s, most of the nations of Western Europe had attained the highest economic capacity in their histories while their workers had reached a level of well-being never thought possible. Welfare and economic development had not flourished at each other's expense but rather had climbed in tandem. What had long been considered an inherent conflict had suddenly transformed itself in a firm and vigorous symbiosis.

Many factors played a role in bringing about this curious, if not revolutionary, change. Rising wage rates had forced capitalists to innovate continuously and to rationalize their operations to the utmost. Welfare benefits such as socialized medicine improved physical and mental well-being, thereby reducing absenteeism and increasing productivity. In one of the first French factories to pay workers full compensation for time missed in sickness, absenteeism went down by 50 percent while total employee productivity rose by nearly 3 percent. Fringe benefits induced some forced savings from both sides which could be, and was invested. More importantly, such welfare benefits maintained purchasing power and kept small dips in the business cycle from becoming big ones. Full employment policies kept manpower resources from going to waste, while the dislocations caused by the war greatly increased worker mobility. All this is not to deny the vital role played by Marshall Plan funds in Europe's economic resurgence. However, by the early 1950s, such assistance came to an end while the Old World's economic boom continued to roll forward.

This positive correlation between welfare and growth, and even between welfare and capitalist profits, becomes still more evident when we compare the Western European nations with each other. During most of the postwar period, France and West Germany spurred ahead of Great Britain in economic growth. At the same time, France and Germany disbursed larger proportions of their national income on welfare. In 1960, for example, West Germany spent 10.4 percent and France spent 8.3 percent of their respective gross national products (GNP) on welfare. Britain's expenditure for this purpose the same year amounted to only 6.4 percent of its GNP.

Looking still further, we find that French employers were contributing 69 percent and West German employers were contributing 41 percent of social security revenue in their respective countries. Their British counterparts, however, were doling out a mere 21 percent of their nation's social security income. Yet French and German employers were enjoying fatter, or at least faster growing, profits. Economists had long been fond of quoting the Biblical maxim: To him who hath shall be given. Now it became necessary to add a corollary: To him who gives shall be given.

Carrying the comparison between Great Britain and the Continent still further enables us to shatter another prewar truism regarding capitalist economics and to illuminate a further dimension of the new convergence. It had long been taken for granted that unemployment was an effective way of controlling inflation. Consequently, a certain amount of joblessness was considered desirable and at times even necessary to keep the capitalist ship on an even keel. However, while Britain during much of the postwar period maintained an unemployment level that was two to three times that of West Germany, the island country failed to achieve a price advantage over her former enemy. If anything, the reverse proved true. In this country, meanwhile, the Eisenhower administration experienced a much higher unemployment rate than the Kennedy–Johnson administrations which followed it. But the latter sustained a lower level of inflation.

When we cast our gaze northward to Sweden, the fatherland of welfarism, we find further confirmation of this convergence. During most of the 1960's, Sweden's growth rate exceeded that of France and Germany. At the same time, its workers remained the highest paid in Europe and enjoyed, for the most part, the highest level of welfare benefits. Swedish capitalists do not express any desire to alter this situation fundamentally. They continually point out to foreign interviewers that the country's social welfare system has meant increased rather than decreased profits. Furthermore, while inflation has certainly not been unknown in Sweden's postwar experience, it would be difficult to claim that it has caused economic damage through pricing Swedish goods too high. During the 1960s, Sweden, with only one four-hundredths of the world's population accounted for approximately one-fortieth of the world's exports.*

Although the growth rates of the Western European nations have generally exceeded our own during the past quarter-century, they have themselves been surpassed by another industrialized country, Japan. This remarkable land has maintained an economic growth pattern in recent years of around 13 to 14 percent and in some earlier years it managed to do even better. Since Japanese wage scales seem significantly lower than those of Western Europe, does this mean that capitalism still thrives best when its workers' incomes are supressed? Does the Japanese phenomenon refute the thesis of the new convergence?

The answer to this question must be no. First of all, Japanese wage

---

* In 1970, the Nixon administration tried to curb inflation by policies which also brought rising unemployment. While these steps may have had some value as a short-term measure, their potential for boomeranging soon became apparent. The American economy, for a while, stopped growing, and by the Fall of 1970, the system was confronted with strident demands for wage increases but with little increased productivity to absorb them.

levels are by no means so low as they appear at first glance. The Committee for Economic Development (CED) took a long and careful look at the total compensation paid to Japanese workers in the mid-1960s and concluded that Japan's startling resurgence was not being made at the expense of the country's work force. When all the benefits which Japanese workers receive are weighed in the balance, the scales are not as tipped to one side as is often claimed. "It seems clear that comprehensive figures would not show Japanese labor costs, per hour of work, to be so low as is suggested by the comparison of regular wages alone," noted the CED. Furthermore, according to the Committee, even those advantages which Japan may have possessed in this area are substantially, if not wholly, offset by higher costs for capital and raw materials.

Japan's extraordinary economic growth has been largely due not to low worker remuneration but to high worker productivity. A ship that takes 450,000 man hours to produce in the United States requires only 320,000 man hours in Japan. While the average American steelworker in the late 1960s was producing 150 tons a year, his Japanese colleague was turning out 200 tons a year.

Far from disproving the theory that worker welfarism is congruent with productivity and therefore capitalist profit, the Japanese experience seems to amplify and strengthen it. Japanese workers actually enjoy more coddling than those of any other country. No matter how low or high he may be on the organizational totem pole, the Japanese wage earner enjoys almost complete job security. Unless he commits a fairly major crime, he is almost never fired. Furthermore, Japanese firms almost never attempt to undertake any systematic evaluation of an employee's ability or output. Promotion in terms of title and salary is generally awarded strictly on the basis of seniority. In other words, Japanese personnel systems incorporate what we in this country believe to be the most wasteful and efficiency-deterring feature of our worst civil service systems. Yet, in Japan, complete adherence to tenure and seniority has failed to prevent and may have even encouraged the highest levels of worker productivity in the world!

Several leading economists have noticed this growing consistency of worker welfarism with economic growth and capitalist earnings. The British economists Eric Roll and Andrew Schonfield have both called attention to this development. As Schonfield has pointed out, "Full employment and the enhanced bargaining power of wage earners have not resulted in the diversion of resources away from investment, which is heavily dependent on profits for its financing, and into personal consumption. In fact, the level of domestic investment, measured as a proportion of gross national product, was notably higher in the 1950s than in any comparable period in the first half of the twentieth century in all West European countries for which records exist." In this country, the new convergence has been colorfully summed by John Beckett, president of the huge Transamerica Corporation. "More pay for less work, that's the new American way. It could drive us all to the rich house."

Yet, despite the mounting pile of evidence regarding the growth of employer–employee interest convergence, vexing questions remain and nagging doubts persist. Are not workers still exploited? Don't the owners still skim off the cream leaving the actual producers with far less than they deserve? And isn't this borne out by the fact that the proportion of the national income going to the work force has remained largely the same, at least in most countries?

The question of income disparity and its persistence or nonpersistence does not lend itself to easy answers, but there is certainly some evidence to indicate that income inequality tends to shrink in the more developed stages of industrialization. This can be seen even in the United States where the income gap between those at the top and those at the bottom of the economy has been greater than in many European welfare states. Focusing on the United States, we find the following factors at work:

1. The proportion of the national income going to wages has risen fairly steadily during the past 50 years. According to figures prepared by economist Bernard F. Haley of Stanford University, employee compensation absorbed 53.2 percent of the national income from 1910 to 1919. By fits and starts, it gradually rose to where it was consuming 70 percent of the national income during the 1954–1963 period. Since then, it appears to have grown even more. My own calculations show that while proprietors' income went up 16 percent and corporation profits rose by 35 percent from 1963 to 1968, employee compensation increased by 41 percent.

2. Within the work force itself, there has been, as we have seen, a dramatic growth in professional employees. The salaries of professionals and semiprofessionals are closer or at least less remote from management salaries than are the salaries of the blue collar and white collar cleri-

cal employees whom they are replacing. As the work force becomes more professional, the gap between its compensation and that of its managers tends to shrink.

3. Even within the managerial salary structure itself, wage scales have tended to flatten. A study by the well-known management consulting firm McKinsey and Company shows that between 1956 and 1967, the pay of the top 1 percent of executives rose 23 percent. But during the same period, the pay of the bottom 30 percent of business executives rose 54 percent, or more than twice as much.

4. Within the entire economy, public employment has risen at a much faster rate than private employment and public employees now make up nearly 20 percent of the labor force. Income disparity is far less in the public sector than in the private sector. A top level federal executive may earn five or six times as much as his secretary; his colleague in business may earn 50 to 60 times as much as his secretary. Thus, a relative increase in public versus private employment tends automatically to reduce income disparity in the population. It should further be noted that within the public sector itself, employment in state and local government has risen faster than in the federal government and income differences are even less at the state or local level. A municipal or even state commissioner may earn no more than three or four times the pay of his secretary and sometimes even less than that.

5. The proportion of the gross national product expended for public goods has steadily risen through the years. Only 7 percent of the nation's output was consumed by government in 1929. By the mid-1950s, government spending was eating up one-quarter of the nation's GNP and by 1970, the figure was nearing the one-third mark.

While abuses certainly occur, public expenditures do tend to redistribute income in a more equalizing manner. This was particularly true during the 1960s when expenditures for such things as welfare and public education rose far more rapidly than expenditures for such things as highways and defense. In percentage terms the proportion of the federal budget devoted to human resources rose from 30 to 41 percent from fiscal 1961 to fiscal 1971. The proportion of the federal budget earmarked for defense dropped from 48 to 37 percent during the same period. And this shift occurred despite the fact that we were fighting a war during the latter year. (Defense spending is expected to remain stable at most and probably will decline during the 1970s and, if the total level of government spending keeps on rising, as seems inevitable, then the proportion of both government expenditure and gross national product devoted to defense will decline even more.) Furthermore, state and local spending increased more rapidly than federal spending and so the proportional decline of defense expenditure in the overall government expenditure pattern was even greater than what is obtained from looking at the federal figures alone.

6. The American tax structure, despite the persistence of numerous inequities, has become somewhat more progressive in recent years. During the 1960s, more and more state and local governments began shifting toward income taxes. From 1968 to 1969, for instance, total state revenues rose by 14 percent while total state revenues from income taxes alone rose by 20 percent. Though state and local income taxes are usually less progressive than the federal government's, they are none the less usually more progressive than the sales and property taxes which they have been supplanting. At the national level, meanwhile, Congress in 1969 enacted, and the President signed, a modified tax reform plan which somewhat strengthened the progressivity of the federal income tax system. Oil depletion allowances were cut back, a ceiling on the amount of untaxed income a person could claim as untaxed was established, and dependency deduction allowances which help the lower income groups particularly were raised.

For these reasons, the United States does appear to be moving, hesitantly and haltingly to be sure, but moving just the same, toward greater income equality. Nearly every agenda item for the 1970s indicates that the trend will not only continue but will accelerate. The coming decade should see further tax reform, more assistance to public education, increased welfare allowances (President Nixon's welfare plan is before the Congress as this is written), more rebuilding of slums, stepped-up employee and citizen participation in economic enterprise (to be discussed at greater length later in this chapter), and increasing professionalization of the work force. All these developments point to further and possibly quite dramatic narrowing of the income gap in the coming years.*

We are now left with the most fundamental question of all, namely

---

* Sufficient data are not available, at least to this writer, to prove that income equalization is going forward in other countries. But such data as are available do indicate such a trend in most developed countries. One exception—there may be others—is West Germany. However, the German Parliament has already enacted legislation designed to bring about some redistribution of the country's wealth and further legislation is being considered.

the question of labor exploitation. The sweat shops of yesteryear may have passed from the scene, but do not private employers derive their earnings from the surplus produced by the employees? And isn't it in the interest of these employees to try to take back as much of this surplus as possible, making themselves considerably richer and leaving the owners with nothing at all?

Gardiner C. Means examines this question in his preface to the revised edition of *The Modern Corporation and Private Property*, the landmark work which he coauthored with Adolph Berle more than 30 years ago. In this new preface, Means notes that in 1967, the last year for which he had figures, only 12 percent of corporate income went to capital. Of this 12 percent, more than half went to reinvestment, that is growth. Of the less than half that was left for interest and dividends, a larger proportion was paid in income taxes than was paid by wages and salaries, since bondholders and stockholders, for the most part, are in higher tax brackets than are workers and employees. He thus concluded that if all 12 percent of capital's return, less the amount needed for taxes and investment, went to labor, then worker compensation, even after allowing for management salaries, could not have been increased more than 3 or 4 percent. "In the light of an increase in real wage rates of about 3 percent a year," said Means, "it is difficult to find a great deal of exploitation here." *

CONVERGENCE AND THE NEW ADMINISTRATION

We are now left with what is for our purposes the most basic question of all: does this new convergence extend into the administrative arena? If we examine any specific work situation—and here we are talking about public as well as private administration—will we not find that employees will want to work less and earn more while managers will seek the opposite? Are not the basic desires and tendencies, if not the inherent motivations, of superior and subordinates usually at odds if not at war?

To answer this question let us first turn back to Japan. It will be recalled that in Japan, employees enjoy almost absolute employment

---

* My own calculations indicate that if he could have used 1968 or 1969 figures, he would have come out with an even smaller "exploitation" rate.

protection, not just in terms of job security but also in terms of promotion and advancement. Yet, as we saw, such a system has been consistent with, if not actually promotive of, the highest employee productivity levels in the world. This seemingly anomalous state of affairs may be thought to be a peculiarly Japanese or Oriental phenomenon that has no bearing on Western culture and experience. However, a closer look at Europe indicates that such is not the case. England's economic growth and general economic experience, it will be recalled, has generally failed to equal that of France and Germany during most of the postwar period. At the same time, it was also noted that employee benefits in Great Britain have fallen far short of those enjoyed by workers on the Continent. If we delve somewhat further, we will find that this discrepancy covers job protection and other administrative elements in the work situation.

As Schonfield has pointed out, the French worker, in contrast to his British colleague, enjoyed during the 1950s and 1960s the right by law to one month notice or severance pay after six months on a job and the right to sue his employer if the latter dismissed him without good reason. The German worker fared even better. He could, for example, collect up to 95 percent of his income in unemployment benefits and was entitled to full workman's compensation even for injuries that were in no way work connected. Once retired, he could, after 1957, count on a pension that would continually be adjusted upward not only to meet increases in the cost of living but also to give him his share of the country's economic growth.

Sweden's remarkable economic history offers further proof that administrative as well as economic welfarism is conducive to worker productivity and capitalist profit.

These European and Japanese experiences suggest that the new convergence has an administrative as well as an economic dimension. A host of studies and investigations conducted in this country over the past few decades substantiate and amplify such a claim.

The first point of interest brought to light by this research is the simple but often neglected fact that people basically want to work. For example, one study cited by Harry Levinson showed that of a nationwide sample of 400 men employed at various occupations, 80 percent said they would prefer to continue working even if they were to inherit enough money to live comfortably. Quite possibly a portion of the remaining 20 percent might also return to the work force once they had tasted the tempting but often dubious joys of inaction. This pattern of response cannot be attributed to any unique American cultural trait. France, for instance, has never been considered a nation with a strongly imbued work ethic, but a study of French pensioners showed that a majority would have preferred to have continued being employed.

The second noteworthy fact which has emerged from the mounting pile of research into employee-management relations is the comparative weakness of purely economic motives. Fritz J. Roethlisberger has summed up these findings in these words:

> Whenever and wherever this assumption (that people are primarily motivated by economic interests) has been seriously investigated in the light of facts, its universal validity has been seriously questioned. Investigator after investigator has agreed on this point: Far from being the prime and sole mover of human activity in business, economic interest has run far behind in the list of incentives that make men willing to work.

The third fact which has emerged to support the convergence theory is the desire of people not only to work but to do work that is useful and productive. Dostoyevsky once said that the surest way to destroy a man is to render his work useless. Alan Harrington has pointed out that almost no one, no matter how highly he was paid, would or could permanently dig holes in the ground and fill them up afterwards. Human beings are fundamentally motivated to do what employers want them to do: produce.

Further studies only add detail and substance to this picture of convergence. Among the things they indicate are the following:

1. Skilled workers in general and knowledge workers in particular derive their greatest job satisfaction *from a feeling of work accomplishment*. Recognition by their employers runs only a poor second in their reward hierarchy, while financial remuneration places still farther down the list.
2. When workers think they are overpaid, they tend to work harder to make up for it.
3. When work standards and performance levels are high, worker satisfaction increases. When such standards and performance levels are low, and when supervision is lax or indifferent, worker satisfaction goes down.

However, although workers react negatively to lax and indifferent supervision, this does not mean that they crave directive control and it certainly does not mean that they want to be viewed primarily in terms of their productivity. And it is not in management's best interest to do so either. According to Edward and Gladys Ogden Dimock, "Research generally confirms . . . that productivity is higher when supervisors are emyloyee-oriented than when they are production-oriented and authority is rigidly centralized." As an example of such research, a study of 24 clerical sections in an insurance company showed that productivity was lower in those sections that were closely supervised than in those sections where employees were given more discretion to work in their own way.

Sociologist Peter Blau in citing this study, notes that "Supervisors who were primarily concerned with maintaining a high level of production, interestingly enough, were less successful in meeting this goal than those supervisors who were more interested in the welfare of their subordinates than in sheer production; in the latter case, productivity was generally higher."

Thus convergence is an integral part of the new administration as it is of the new economics. This convergence, to be sure, is not always fully perceived and appreciated by either side. It is also more fully developed in knowledge work situations than in others. However, as the results of the various studies become increasingly known and as knowledge workers increasingly replace blue collar and clerical white collar workers, we shall see it playing an ever greater role in management–employee relations. It is both a spur to, and a goal of, the administrative revolution.

CONTOURS OF CONVERGENCE: TRADE UNIONISM

Shortly after the 1968 general strike had nearly shattered the French economy, the president of the Center of Young Business Executives of France recorded himself and his organization as firmly and unequivocally in favor of strong trade unions. In the light of France's bitter and bloody history of union-management conflict, of which the "events of May" was merely the latest episode, his statement seemed puzzling and surprising. But Pierre Bellon was in dead earnest. Speaking for the organization which represents the future of French capitalism, he called for a stronger and more vigorous trade union movement that would encompass an increasing number of French workers.

"Why are we partisans of strong trade unions?" asked Bellon. After pointing out that this was not a new position for the younger French capitalists but went back some five years, he presented two reasons for their seemingly unorthodox attitude.

"In the first place, it is necessary to recognize that social progress has only taken place in France thanks to the activity of the unions. Second, we have found that the countries which are most advanced economically . . . are those countries where trade unionism is well-organized and powerful. There seems, therefore, to exist a rapport between economic efficiency and union effectiveness."

The parallel development of trade unionism and economic abundance which Bellon notes is borne out by most available data and can certainly not be ascribed to mere coincidence. Those European countries with the strongest and most united trade unions do seem to be the ones whose capitalists are enjoying the greatest economic blessings.

There are many reasons why this is so. First, in securing welfare benefits for their members the unions advance the employee's sense of well-being and security. This, in turn, allows and encourages him to become more productive. MacGregor continually emphasized the necessity of giving the employee a sense of security at the outset of his employment and not making it a reward for his work performance. This, he argued, will reduce the employee's sense of dependency and permit him to work more productively. The trade union, MacGregor noted, can help create this desired situation and thereby clear the decks for a more productive relationship between the employee and the organization.

Unions, of course, do seem to harass management but even this can promote management's interests. If there is discord and dissension in the ranks, stemming, say, from middle management abuses, the unions will often bring this to the attention of the top in time for the problems involved to be resolved. Unions provide a valuable means of communication between the various levels and sectors of an organization and while not all problems are correctable by improved communication, many of them are.

Even the union's pressures for increased wages can benefit those who must pay them. Such pressures frequently force management to innovate and rationalize its activities, thus spurring progress and helping prevent stagnation and decay. And by forestalling the erosion of work-ars' wages in bad times, unions help curtail a dampening of purchasing power that could turn a slow-down into a depression. It became apparent in the United States in the early 1930s, for example, that the depression was "feeding on itself."

As economies mature, and union-management contacts increase, there is a tendency for unions and employers to work more and more co-operatively. MacGregor compared the growth of such cooperation to the maturation process. Each has to go through an adolescent phase, he said, until they eventually understand their mutual interests. When unions finally learn that there is not that much of a surplus available for redistribution, they tend to shift their efforts. Instead of focusing entirely on obtaining a bigger slice of the *existing* pie, they start thinking of trying to help create a *bigger* pie.

Instances of such cooperation abound in the chronicles of labor-management relations. As early as 1941, the Joint Board of the Dress-makers Union of the International Ladies Garment Workers Union offered employers a cooperative program for modernizing the New York dress industry. The Amalgamated Clothing Workers Union for many years has operated a management consulting service to aid struggling clothing factories. The well-known profit-sharing system known as the Scanlon Plan was conceived by a union leader as a way in which the employees could help a company survive. It has proven its worth in an increasing number of instances.

As workers, responding to high employment and high wages, become more independent, the union tends to become management's best and sometimes only means of control. "There is more than one industry today," writes Elie Ginzberg, "where the employer has practically no disciplinary power left. The trade union alone keeps rein on the unruly and inefficient." It is common, in talking with business leaders these days, to hear them express the wish that the unions in their plants were more, rather than less, powerful. As Dale Wassermann, an official of the State, County, and Municipal Employees Union points out, "The same management types who were screaming about 'the overlords of labor' back during the McClellan hearings are now the ones screaming about 'labor anarchy.'"

Sweden has perhaps the most powerful and most unified trade union organization in the world and this has proven a boon to labor, man-agement, and the nation. The union helps handle problems as they occur and keeps brush fires from developing into major conflagrations. Since one union organization can speak for nearly the whole work force, it is possible for employers to negotiate long-term and comprehensive contracts and then make their adjustment and plans for the future with comparative certainty as to what their labor problems and expenses will be. At the same time, the fact that the trade union movement represents the interests of virtually all workers and thereby most of the public prompts the labor organization to accept and even welcome measures which an individual union might spurn. The phasing out of unprofitable industries, the adoption of time and motion studies, and other such steps are accepted and often encouraged by Sweden's national labor organization since the overall gains that could result to the economy bring overall gains to the work force.

The emergence of unions as a main lever of labor control and as partners in the furtherance of economic growth has produced a further development indicative of the new convergence. At one time, employers not only resisted unionism in general but opposed industrial unionism most of all. If business leaders had to accept unionism, then they preferred to deal with numerous craft unions whom they could frequently play against one another rather than bargain with an industrial union that could shut down an entire plant or even an entire industry with one blow of the whistle. During the 1930s, employers consistently tended to favor the craft-based A.F.L. over the industrially-oriented C.I.O. for this reason.

But the times they are a-changin' and now employers are starting to switch their preferences to industrial unions even though such unions are more powerful and can speak for their members with a stronger voice. Craft unions, it is felt, tend to perpetuate old skills and old procedures. They reduce labor mobility and flexibility. They also generate intra-industrial rivalries and conflicts which, management is finding, tend to hurt them as well as the workers.

United Auto Workers' late president Walter Reuther persuaded the American military government in Germany after World War II to organize industrial unions rather than seek to restore the former craft guilds. In so doing, he helped set the stage for a prosperous German capitalism. British unionism, on the other hand, failed to go through such a transformation and this has started to play havoc with the country's economic development. Approximately 90 percent of the more than 3,000 strikes which broke out in Britain during 1969 were wildcat walkouts and many of them were caused by jurisdictional disputes between warring craft unions. The emergence of strong industrial unions in Great Britain would be a boon to all concerned, including, of course, the public.

In this country, much of the unease and anxiety caused by unions in recent years emanates from the public sector. President Kennedy issued a presidential order in 1962 giving exclusively-recognized trade unions the right to bargain collectively with the federal government. Since then, the number of unionized federal employees has grown apace, reaching 54 percent of the federal work force at the start of 1970. Unionism among state and local government workers has scored nearly commensurate advances.

Many see an anomaly and a danger in this trend. The idea of employees forming unions to bargain with nonprofit public agencies seems inconsistent with the public interest. And the fact that a rash of public employee strikes has accompanied this union growth does little to allay their fears. Public employees are, at least to some extent, free of the economic checks which curtail the militancy of workers in industry. The services of public employees are usually indispensable for, unlike a private firm, a public agency can rarely shut down for any extended period of time. Furthermore, there is no rigid limit on what they can demand or obtain since their employers don't have to make a profit to remain in business.

There would seem to be a potential for peril here, but fortunately, it has generally, though not always, remained more potential than actual. Public employees have a greater identity of interest with their employers and with the public generally than do their fellow-toilers in the private economy. They are not only subject to legal sanctions but political and social ones as well. The last may prove particularly effective because public employees have to live amidst their employer's customers, and since the services they provide for these customers are usually vital and exclusive, the latter are quick to respond with hostility when such services are suspended. Indeed, public employees themselves, along with their families, are in most cases clients for the same services they provide.

Public employee unions have tended to play a constructive role in the operations of the public sector. They have helped to resolve problems and foster improvement. Their role performance in this area is often obscured by more sensational and more newsworthy eruptions of conflict. But such positive activities more often than not constitute the bulk of union activity in a public agency once management has become reconciled to the union's existence and learned to live with it.

The best examples of such cooperative activity in the public sector are drawn from Western Europe where public employee unionism has developed an older history and secured a greater acceptability than in the United States. A good case in point is the public agency whose growing involvement in unionism in this country has caused the most qualms, the police.

In 1966, I spent several months in Western Europe doing research on police behavior and administration. While in Sweden, the director of that country's police force, Carl Persson told me that "it would not be possible for us to work effectively without the union." He elaborated by pointing out that the union facilitates the working out of problems and the implementation of new ideas. Just one year previously, Sweden had combined all her local police departments into one national police force and, according to Persson, the union had helped tremendously in effecting such a sweeping reorganization.

A month later, while interviewing the then deputy prefect of the Paris Police, Roland Fougere, I repeated Persson's statement and asked for his comment. Fougere generally agreed with his Swedish colleague. The unions, he noted, often "wake us up and make us look at situations which we have not known of or have neglected. They also permit a dialogue between the rank and file and the administration. Finally, they spur professionalism." (It should be kept in mind that neither Persson nor Fougere are professional policemen; it is customary in most European countries to appoint only civilian administrators to head police agencies.)

As I continued researching the subject, I came across numerous examples to back up the somewhat strange stance which these police officials had adopted. Police union periodicals in most of these countries carried articles and columns on the latest judicial rulings, new police techniques, and other professionally useful items of information. Also, the demands that police unions made and the information they disclosed seemed, for the most part, to serve the public interest. In the former category was the demand by the Swedish police union that the administration increase police education and expand police public relations activity in order to strengthen the relationship between the police and the public. In the latter category was a press conference by the head of the German police union in which he disclosed that German detectives were simply not investigating all burglary cases. Nearly everyone I interviewed, including academicians and journalists, firmly agreed that the police unions had helped to make the police both more efficient and more democratic.

In this country, public employee unionism is still in its infancy and in most areas has not yet chalked up the long record of positive achievement which such unions in Europe have compiled. Yet there have already been indications that American public employee unionism is heading in this direction.

Late in 1968, a federal employee union protested the existence of a "back door" hiring system which allowed retired military officers to circumvent civil service procedures in obtaining public employment. The Civil Service Commission admitted the problem and set about to correct it. In New York, a newly organized union of correction officers took the lead in exposing what it called "nineteenth century conditions" in the city's penal institutions. It demanded constructive change. The New York City teachers union has logged an impressive record in furthering progressive and liberal educational reform. The union staffed the Freedom Schools of Virginia and Mississippi, encouraged and aided the city's school board in developing a program for recruiting and training minority group teachers, proposed a Parent Review Board, and sought the creation of standards of accountability in order to raise the level of teaching in the city. Furthermore, though considered to be opposed to decentralization for its stand against certain actions by the administrator of a model decentralized school district, the teachers union had actually supported the law which had created the district.

Despite its record of positive accomplishment in improving the delivery of educational services in New York City, the United Federation of Teachers is still best known for its long and powerful strike against the city's school system in the fall of 1968. And this strike is only one of many such walkouts by teachers and other public employees that occurred as soon as unionism began to make headway in the public sector during the 1960s. Does the parallel rise in public employee strikes and public employee unionism mean that unionism leads to strikes and the breakdown of public services?

To answer this, we should just note that public employee strikes have a long history in the United States. In 1940, Columbia University Press published a book entitled *One Thousand Strikes of Government Employees*. Written by David Ziskind, a United States Department of Labor official, it showed that walkouts had already become a not uncommon occurrence in the public sector. Yet, there was, at this time, little public employee unionism. The rash of strikes which accompanied the growth of government employee unions in the 1960s is due not to the unions themselves but to the conditions which gave rise to both them and the strikes, namely an increasing sense of frustration by public employees.

Two rather jolting public service strikes which occurred in North America during 1969 serve to buttress this contention. Both the Montreal police strike in Canada and the postal service strike in the United States began as wildcat walkouts. The unions only sanctioned them after they had already begun. At the same time, the union leadership in both cases seems to have played an important role in keeping these outbreaks from deepening and enduring. Unions, it should be noted, tend to dislike strikes because they drain union treasuries and generally weaken union control. Thus, the growth of such public employee associations has probably prevented more strikes than it has caused. It is interesting to note that Canada has given certain of its public service unions the right to strike and this has produced less rather than more labor-management conflict. In this country, two states, Hawaii and Pennsylvania, have given teachers the right to strike. They have been, among urbanized states, the least bothered by teachers' strikes.

Then there is the question of how damaging strikes really are. Though the suspension of education, sanitation, and other public services does constitute a severe threat to the workings of industrialized and urbanized society, nevertheless many, and perhaps most strikes have produced benefits which exceed their costs. The costs, in terms of school days lost, garbage not picked up, etc., is rarely irremediable, while the clearing of the air and the resolution of the problems which the strike usually though not always produces may provide long-lasting improvement. The Los Angeles teachers union settled its spring 1970 strike solely on the basis of improvements in the educational system. In securing such changes, the teachers passed up a 5 percent pay raise which the Board of Education had offered them.

MacGregor, in claiming that unions and management naturally tend towards cooperation if not collaboration, was careful to point out that this may not be true in the beginning stages of their relationship. Discontent and frustration often provide the impetus for unionization, he noted, and, as a result, the union's first leaders will often be those who can yell the loudest. Frequently, the union's first aim is revenge. However, once the union has firmly established itself and once management has fully recognized it, the stage is set for a pattern of constructive and mutually beneficial interaction. This evolution has, for the most part, already occurred in the public sector of many Western European nations and eventually should take place in our country as well. However, its advent will probably require the granting of a new right by management and the assumption of a new responsibility by employees. This right and this responsibility is participation.

CONTOURS OF CONVERGENCE: PARTICIPATION

The governments that took office in Western Europe after World War II came under pressure not only to democratize their societies but to democratize themselves. The old bureaucratic way of handling government employees would no longer suffice. Newer methods were demanded and the major change which emerged was increased employee participation.

Such employee participation in the public sector had not been unknown. Great Britain had moved to set up the Whitely Councils back in World War I as a way of giving workers in both government and industry some say in the decisions which affect them. While this pioneering step had met with more indifference than enthusiasm in the private sector, it managed to secure a foothold in government. Before World War II, Sweden had also given some recognition to the participatory concept.

Following the second World War, the participatory movement suddenly blossomed. Those countries that already had begun to move in this direction began to accelerate their efforts. Those countries which had never set up participatory institutions began to do so.

In France, this drive for employee participation in government gave birth to the *commissions administratif paritaire* or round-table commissions. These bodies are made up of equal numbers of rank and file employees elected by their colleagues and of officials appointed by the administration, with a chairman designated by the administration. They now exist throughout the French bureaucracy and decide many personnel matters such as promotions, disciplinary actions, etc.

West Germany responded to this new trend by establishing *personal-*

räten or personnel boards. Composed of three employees chosen by the rank and file, they handle employee grievances of all kinds. In larger government units, board members are released from their jobs and given office space and secretarial help to carry out their duties.

Belgium decided to integrate public service employee unions into the machinery of government by setting up a joint central commission as well as joint central committees for each ministry. These union committees have the right to be consulted on all questions affecting personnel, organization of work, conditions of service, and questions of hygiene and security.

In many cases, informal arrangements have grown up which permit these institutions to transcend their prescribed boundaries. For example, it has now become customary for some Scandinavian police departments to clear all their appointments of officers with the unions involved. And during the late 1950s and early 1960s a German police commissioner named Fredrick Schafer turned over to his personnel board virtually the entire task of making officer appointments. His arrangement apparently worked well, for Schafer's political fortunes began to rise. His party, the Social Democrats, chose him as a candidate for parliament and eventually made him their floor leader in the national legislature.

Needless to say, the private sector could not and did not remain immune from this new trend. In some cases, participation in business and industry went beyond the levels established in government. Again, Sweden helped lead the way. A 1946 agreement between the Swedish union federation and the employers association provided the basis for setting up work councils in all enterprises employing 25 or more persons. They are composed of management and union members in equal numbers and meet at least four times a year. Management is obligated to supply the council with a full range of information on finances, inventory, profits, market outlook, etc., and to consult with the council on all major policy decisions. However, the councils have no powers of decision and the unions have preferred to keep it that way. They feel that the decisions should be made by management who would then bear the complete responsibility.

A few years after the Swedish arrangement was conceived, the German unions decided to go their Nordic comrades one better. They asked for, and obtained, a codetermination law giving workers, through freely-elected representatives, a direct say in the formulation of company policy. In these industries affected by the codetermination law—chiefly iron, steel and coal—workers not only elect a work council to handle matters directly affecting them but also elect one-third of the company's board of directors.

Codetermination has not been an unqualified success in Germany. Up to now low worker interest in, and low worker knowledge of, economic and financial matters has curbed employee participation in these areas of company policy. But in terms of personnel matters and questions involving workers directly, the organs of codetermination have accomplished a good deal. The German coal industry has undergone some painful changes since World War II. Many mines and plants have shut down and many workers have been forced to take training for other positions. Codetermination has helped to ease and facilitate this transition.

Juris Alksnitis, a student of the participation movement, says, "On the whole, work councils must be considered a success. Not only have they demonstrated that employees can participate in managerial functions, but also that a genuine spirit of collaboration between employees and management can be developed."

The participatory movement in the French and British private sectors, meanwhile, remains stunted and undeveloped. Although both countries have woven considerable employee participation into their governmental operations, and although both provide certain specific instances of successful participation in private firms—instances which we will examine later—participation in business and industry has lagged in both countries.

In France, this has occurred despite rather determined efforts by the government to further such a concept. During his ten-year reign, Charles de Gaulle came to view worker participation in both profits and decision-making as a way to break out of the bitter class struggle which had for so long characterized and hampered French society. The de Gaulle government enacted legislation authorizing plant committees composed of labor and management representatives to be established in all industrial and commercial enterprises employing 50 or more persons. The committees were designed, however, to be only consultative and more often than not failed even to fulfill this modest role.

Many factors peculiar to French culture exist to explain this failure of participation to make much general headway so far. Alksnitis notes that "Long traditions of family ownership and authoritarian administration contribute to employer distrust of worker intentions. Therefore, although committees are supposed to be consulted on issues economic and technical in nature, management response has been less than co-operative. Information from management is often incomplete, late or not rendered at all for 'security' reasons. On the other hand, the unions, particularly the communist-dominated ones, have been known to disclose business secrets discussed in committee meetings."

Committee participation in technical matters has been more successful, but even here it falls far short of achieving its potential. Says Alksnitis, "Major technical matters frequently remain the prerogative of special staffs; minor suggestions do not encourage continued initiative." The one area where the plant committees have scored major breakthroughs, Alksnitis concludes, is in social-welfare problems.

In the wake of the French general strike of 1968, however, fresh winds are stirring. The French Parliament's Committee on Social, Cultural and Family Affairs held a series of hearings on the subject of participation shortly after the strike and the testimony makes impressive reading. Representatives of both management and labor organizations showed up to affirm their commitment to strengthening and enhancing the participatory concept. The only negative witnesses were the spokesmen for small business and for the communist labor unions. And even the latter two groups felt constrained to admit some validity to the notion. Of course, there is often a large gap between words and deeds, but the tenor of the testimony and the events that have transpired since then indicate that the participatory notion is slowly, and with fits and starts, beginning to take hold in French business thinking.

Britain's private sector remains an even greater holdout in joining this trend. Stodgy managements, bickering craft unions, and too many years of Tory rule have made participation the exception rather than the rule in industrial and commercial operations. However, there are exceptions, and interesting ones, as we shall soon see.

What about Japan? This unique country, despite the patriarchal nature of much of its industrial management, makes extensive use of participation. However, this is carried out in informal and often quite subtle ways. In the view of many observers, decisions in Japan are often not made at all. Instead, problems are discussed and bandied about until the decision seems to make itself. In the words of one American businessman who studied Japanese methods, "decisions seep upward from a sort of consensus."

Certain institutional devices do exist for helping make such a system work. One is the "ringsho" or work paper which is circulated to all affected parties and subunits for comments. This allows even those far down the ladder to make some input into the decision-making process. It also enables management to tap a full range of ideas and criticisms and, at the same time, discover just who among its employees have the most promise. Those so discovered are likely to be rewarded with more challenging assignments. Given the nature of Japanese personnel systems, however, such challenges will rarely be accompanied by salary increases or more rapid promotion.

Another participatory device which the Japanese have developed is the quality control circle. This consists of a group of workers who meet regularly to discuss ways of improving their particular product. One quality control circle at Matsushita Electric Company reduced the number of rejects in rice cookers—a key appliance in an Asian country —from 5 in 300 to 1 in 300, or a reduction of 80 percent.

The Japanese also make use of an old American institution called the suggestion box. But in Japanese hands it appears to have reached a level of acceptance and usage that it has rarely, if ever, attained in this country. In some companies, suggestions pour in by the thousands every year and many of them are successfully implemented.

Thus we see that participatory methods have worked and are working in generalized but limited ways in many industrialized countries. There further exists, however, a wide variety of many specific instances of participation being carried to a much more intensive level. A look at some of these will help to indicate the still largely untapped potentialities of this important aspect of the administration revolution.

ISRAEL

One of the first major institutions to carry participation to a higher degree in the modern world has been the Israeli commune or kibbutz. Each kibbutz holds a general meeting every Saturday night—the equivalent of Sunday night in sabbatarian Israel—to determine its goals and operational policies. Not only broad policy matters but also specific directives come in for frequent and often heated debate, with final action taken on the basis of majority vote. It is estimated that 35 to 45 percent of the members take part in any single meeting in older kibbutzim while in more recently established ones as many as 70 percent turn out. The kibbutz administration is in the hands of a secretariat consisting of four to seven elected members. The financial officer and the external relations officer are usually elected for five years but the secretary-general is most often restricted to a two-year term. The old Jacksonian principle of rotation in office is highly esteemed among the kibbutzim and their administrative officials are rarely re-elected to successive terms.

Utilizing wide-scale participation to run an agricultural enterprise is one thing; incorporating such techniques in the operation of industrial plants is another. Yet, the kibbutzim seem to be doing just that. Of the 230 kibbutz communities functioning in Israel at the end of the 1960s, some 170 or nearly three-quarters were operating industrial enterprises. Industrial products now make up nearly half of the total kibbutz output.

Seymour Melman, a professor of industrial engineering at Columbia University, has undertaken a careful study of these cooperatively-run manufacturing firms and come up with some interesting figures. Comparing a sample of the kibbutz firms with a similar sample of privately-owned and operated companies, he found that the cooperative enterprises showed a 26 percent higher productivity of labor, a 67 percent higher productivity of capital, and a 115 percent higher net profit per production worker.

Melman offers many reasons to explain these favorable results. Co-operative control tends to develop in the workers an interest and concern in the firm and its activities which managerially-controlled companies often find hard to generate. The lack of hierarchy encourages a free flow of communication among all members. Furthermore, innovation is encouraged since all tend to share the gains which may result. (There is always plenty of other work available for those whose jobs might be eliminated. And in any case, the kibbutz guarantees security to its members.) There are no wages to pay and therefore no wage administration costs. And the code of consumption equality virtually eliminates labor strife.

The kibbutz enterprise gets a variety of extra work input from its employees in a variety of ways. Melman cites an example:

> Frequently, when some of the administrators or workers of an enterprise eat dinner together in the community dining room and discuss the problems of the work place, this is not an "overtime" task that re-

quires special payment as would be the case in a managerially controlled enterprise where work is done by employees. Though discussion on enterprise problems in the dining hall of the cooperative can be lengthy it is unthinkable to "charge" for this, for there is no theory, category or procedure by which such a "charge" could be made.

YUGOSLAVIA

This Slavic country has encouraged worker-run economic enterprise with increasing economic success. The Galenika Pharmaceutical factory in Belgrade offers an illustration of how this works. The firm is managed by a professional economist but he is chosen, and is responsible to, a 37-member workers council. The members of the council are elected by the firm's 3,000 employees.

Since this form of operation was instituted in the early 1950s, Galenika has steadily grown and prospered. Its total revenues since that time have outstripped its operating costs by some 50 percent. It receives little in the way of government protection and must compete with foreign-made goods not only at home but also in its growing export trade. The workers themselves enjoy a wage that is nearly one-third higher than the Belgrade average. The firm had formerly been a state enterprise and before that time had been a private company. In neither instance had it earned as much or grown as fast as it has under worker control.

Such methods of industrial operation are steadily increasing in Yugoslavia and they are furnishing a tonic to the country's economy. Recent economic growth rates have averaged 8 to 10 percent a year. In 1969, the *National Observer*, a weekly owned and edited by the Wall Street publishing firm of Dow Jones and Company, found that "self-management appears to have allowed Yugoslavia to enjoy an abundance of goods for domestic consumption at the same time it has been giving priority to the development of basic industries." Yugoslavia, concluded the periodical, "is a thriving country."

GERMANY

Dr. Kurt A. Körber, president of the Hauni Werke of Hamburg, has given his 2,000 employees the right to elect by secret ballot their immediate supervisors. He has also granted them seven of the 17 seats on the council he has set up to choose the firm's higher officials. Since a three-quarters majority is required for such appointments, the council has an absolute veto. (The council can also fire him if it wants.) He credits his system with enabling the company to grow from nothing in 1946 to a sales volume of $40 million a year in 1968. It produces machines for making cigarette filters and dominates not only the German but the world market in this field.

Germany's second largest illustrated magazine *Stern* affords another example of successful employee participation in management. Some 150 members of the magazine's editorial staff elect all the members of a seven-man council. This council, by a two-thirds vote, can veto any change in the magazine's ownership as well as any appointment to top editorial positions, including that of the editor-in-chief.

In Essen, meanwhile, Elmar Pieroth, Europe's largest wine dealer, has developed and instituted a plan for giving his 600 employees an opportunity to participate financially in the company. Beginning in 1967, half of the earnings of his company have been earmarked for his employees based on the following formula: 50 percent to all employees on an equal basis and 50 percent allocated on the basis of their yearly wage income. The employees loan the sum back to the company for a five-year period. However, during this time they receive interest at 8 percent per year and at the end of the five years they may convert the loan into stock or redeem it in full for cash.

The 35-year-old Pieroth is a member of the German Parliament and, in cooperation with some of his fellow legislators has worked out a plan to enable all private employees in the country to benefit from financial participation in the enterprises that employ them.

Called Fortune for All (Vermögen für alle) and introduced as a measure into the German Parliament in April 1970, the plan is designed to enable the average worker to acquire a net worth of over $30,000 during a full working life. Since German salaries generally are less than half of those earned by American workers, this sum would be a formidable amount for most of them. It is interesting to note that Pieroth and the other supporters of the plan are all members of the conservative Christian Democratic Party, although the left wing of the Social-Democrats has been demanding a wealth-distribution scheme with increasing stridency.

Francois Sommer, president of Sommer S.A., told the parliamentary committee hearing on participation that his firm had been sharing profits with its workers since 1960. The amounts distributed had already reached the level where they equaled more than one-third of basic salaries. As a result, said Sommer, employees have taken a definite interest in the firm, have produced better goods, and have worked more efficiently. They have also acquired more knowledge of the company and its problems and this has allowed the firm to proceed much more smoothly and much more rapidly with innovation and change.

Another speaker at the same hearing cited an auto parts firm which decided to give its employees half of any increases in its profits. Each of the firm's subunits was assigned its share of the costs and was also provided with a breakdown of the costs of all the other subunits as well. Profits rose from 1,000 francs per employee the first year to 2,000 francs the following year to 3,000 francs the year after that.

In the late 1940s, Ernest Bader created Scott Bader Commonwealth, a resins and plastics firm. He assigned a majority of the stock to the employees under certain stipulations that required them to plow back most of the profits into growth. He also gave the firm's workers extensive powers over personnel procedures including the right to interview and approve applicants for supervisory positions over them. On one occasion, the employees forced Bader to take back a secretary he fired. The firm has prospered in a highly competitive industry, by 1969 employing nearly 400 people with earnings of about $700,000 a year.

In this country, the participation movement has generally been confined to profit-sharing plans. Many of these plans have scored remarkable success. An example of such a success is the Lincoln Electric Company of Cleveland.

Lincoln distributes to its employees all the profit it has left over after it has set aside enough for taxes, investment, and a 6 percent dividend to its stockholders. Its employees have thus become the highest paid in their industry. In addition to earning salaries, which are normal for manufacturing firms in the Cleveland area, they also receive bonuses based on profits and performance which range from 60 to 150 percent of their basic wage.

Yet despite this high compensation, and despite the fact that Lincoln offers guaranteed year-round employment to every employee with at least two years' service, the company's employment costs are low. In an electric machinery company generally, employment costs run 35 percent of sales. At Lincoln, such costs amount to only 25 percent.

Every year the employees elect by secret ballot a 10-member advisory group sometimes referred to as the junior board of directors. This panel meets with management every two weeks to discuss problems and suggest ideas. As might be expected, employee turnover at Lincoln is very low. It amounts to less than 1 percent a year compared with 7 percent for all manufacturing. The total number of employees grew from 1,500 to 2,0000 from 1963 to 1968 and the company is now the world's lafgest manufacturer of arc welding equipment and supplies. Says company founder James F. Lincoln, "We do not distinguish between so-called management and labor. All management must labor and labor must manage."

Substantial worker ownership in this country is still rare but it is increasing. Many companies have inaugurated stock option plans and employees of Sears Roebuck now own nearly 25 percent of the company's shares. Many of the new industries being established in the nation's slums are being organized on the employee-ownership model. And the president of the Chicago and Northwestern Railway, Larry S. Preve, has evolved a plan to turn the railroad which previous managements had bled white over to a new firm whose stock will be entirely owned by the railroad's employees. Preve is betting that such a step produces a rise in operating efficiency that will be sufficient to transform the wobbly railroad into a robust carrier. C. L. Dennis, the head of the Railway and Airline Clerks Union likes the proposal and thinks it will work out.

The 1970s should see a broadening and deepening of the trend toward employee participation. This should prove true in both the public and the private sector and, with regard to the latter, it should encompass both administrative and economic dimensions. The rising proportion of knowledge workers will create a work force that is increasingly inclined to self-motivation and increasingly demanding of decision-making power. This work force will also be increasingly geared to pleasure-deferment and consequently more accepting and desirous of receiving part of its income in the form of long-term investment. Finally, this new work force will be better prepared to grasp the complexities and problems involved in the survival and growth of organizations. It thus will be more able to play active and significant roles in contributing to their prudent operation.

The 1970s started out with a wave of labor unrest gripping many areas of Western society. This unrest seemed most severe in those sectors where participation was weakest. These include the public sector in the United States, the private sector in Britain, and both sectors in Italy. However, increased disruption was making itself felt elsewhere as well. Extended participation seems the needed and necessary antidote to much of this discord. Workers in Germany's iron and steel industries, for example, have turned up on picket lines carrying signs reading "We Demand More Codetermination." This has prompted Chancellor Willy Brandt to remark that "shared decision-making and responsibility in the various areas of society will be a moving force in the years to come." And, he adds, "We are not standing at the end of our democracy; we are only just beginning."

4

THE END OF ORGANIZATION MAN

The publication of *The Organization Man* in 1956 may not have made William Whyte's name a household word but it did manage to achieve such currency for the title of his book. The phrase "organization man" soon became part of the American vocabulary and began cropping up with increasing frequency in writings, speeches, and everyday conversations. Whyte's searing indictment of the growth of organizations, primarily business ones, and the way they were stultifying their members through standards of conformity and cooptation had struck a most responsive chord in American society.

Reviewing this phenomenon from the vantage point of the 1970s, one is impressed with certain of its aspects. For one thing, while Whyte's attack was certainly well-written, well-documented, and interesting, it was not all that new. Observers of the American scene from as far back as the 1830s, when Alexis de Tocqueville visited these shores, had called attention to the forces in American life which tend to create conformity. Domestic writers have been scoring and bewailing such factors ever since. What Whyte found to be typical of American organizations in the 1950s, Sinclair Lewis had found characteristic of American communities in the 1920s. The grim features which Whyte spotlighted and castigated were only the latest manifestation of some long-term trends in American society.

The second noteworthy aspect is the enthusiastic reception which the book received from those establishment institutions which it was attacking. *The New York Times* hailed it as "truly important" and the *Yale Review* described it as "significant."

In this connection, one is impressed by the fact that its writer was an editor of *Fortune* magazine, the nation's foremost spokesman for the business world which bore the brunt of his attack. Not only was *Fortune* apparently unruffled by this withering blast at the institutions it seemingly was sworn to uphold, but the magazine had actually encouraged the author's efforts. In his acknowledgment, Whyte thanked his colleagues on *Fortune*, singling out its managing editor in particular for having given him the time and freedom over a three-year period to enable him to complete his work. Furthermore, Whyte noted that some of his material had already appeared in *Fortune*.

Of course, the American "establishment" has often, though not always, tolerated attacks upon itself. But in this case another factor may well have been at work. Such wholehearted acceptance and support for Whyte's diatribe may well have been caused, or at least facilitated, by the fact that the conditions he was describing and decrying were already on the verge of vanishing. We know from history that revolutions occur when times are becoming better, not worse. A corollary of this may be that an institution becomes most hated and least tolerable just when it is getting ready to pass from the scene. As Eric Hoffer has said, "A grievance is most poignant when almost redressed."

In any case, the constricting and coopting organizations which drew Whyte's scorn and fury were already poised for a fall and since his time, they have been slowly but inexorably undergoing a profound metamorphosis. Whyte's book appeared just as the technological revolution was getting underway and this revolution has little use for organization man. Every year it is making him more and more of an anachronism.

Organization man, we should remember, was essentially George Babbitt in a grey flannel suit. He had somewhat more finesse than Sinclair Lewis' anti-hero; he moved in somewhat more sophisticated circles than the Rotary Club of Zenith. Yet he was essentially a conformist, eager to please peers and superiors, and willing to jettison individualism and integrity in order to get along and to get ahead. While his environmental access had shifted somewhat from the community to the organization, the pressures upon him had remained basically the same. Some of the chapter headings from Whyte's book pointedly illuminated this. "A Generation of Bureaucrats." "The Executive: Non-Well-Rounded Man," "The Fight Against Genius," and "The Bureaucratization of the Scientist."

A variety of factors and forces are causing these chapter headings to become less and less descriptive of organizational life both here and abroad, but before going on to list them, it might be well to point out one element in the situation which was often overlooked. Organization man was never a truly satisfied man. George Babbitt, we will recall, was scarcely a model of relaxed contentment and his counterpart of the 1950s was even less so. While organizational men were submitting to conformist pressures during their work days, they were also spending their evenings hungrily watching TV shows such as westerns which glamorized all the features that their organizational life seemed to lack. Man is not by nature necessarily suited to the role which Whyte described him as fulfilling and, as the reaction to Whyte's book indicates, modern American man was becoming less so all the time.

The first factor to be reckoned with in understanding why organization man has started to pass from the scene of modern society is the emergence of the welfare state. The welfare state drastically curbs the power of organizations to control their members in the manner which Whyte described. It has done so first by maintaining high employment rates and benefit cushions. This enables an employee to be less dependent on any single organization for his livelihood. When jobs are relatively plentiful and people are relatively scarce, people necessarily count for more. And when people know they can always get another job or, if need be, fall back on a cushion of unemployment compensation, they tend to insist on counting for more. In many instances the growth of the welfare state has been accompanied by legislation directly aimed at protecting employees from the type of pressures which Whyte excoriated. This is particularly true in European countries. To cite just one example, a German undertaker in 1961 dismissed a woman employee who insisted, despite repeated warnings, in coming to work in a low-cut pink sweater. She took her case to the German labor court, and under the government's new labor law, the court ordered the employer to pay her damages.

The growth of unionism has also helped curtail organizational coercion. In 1963, the New York Transit Authority (TA) issued a directive specifying that all operating personnel "must be clean shaven while on duty." In 1969, 21 TA employees who insisted on violating this provision by wearing beards were suspended. Their union contested such a step, sought a hearing on the charge, and forced the Transit Authority not only to withdraw the punishment but to rescind the regulation which prompted it.

Then, the growth of public corporations vis-a-vis private corporations has also contributed to this trend. It is much more difficult for a company whose stock is publicly owned and traded than it is for a privately-owned and managed firm to engage in certain forms of arbitrary and capricious behavior. For example, the Allen-Bradley Company cancelled its advertising in the *Saturday Evening Post* when that magazine published an anti-Goldwater editorial in 1964. The Adolph Coors Company gives prospective employees a lie detector test. S. C. Johnson and Son, Incorporated refused to hire married women, except those not living with their husbands, until a 1965 federal law made such discrimination illegal. All these companies are private corporations. No public corporation could ever adopt such policies for it would produce unpleasant attacks on management from at least some stockholders. As public corporations have become a greater and greater part of the private sector, one basis for organizational coercion has correspondingly diminished.

However, it is the growth of knowledge industries which is spearheading the way out of the organizational swampland which Whyte so chillingly depicted. According to Peter Drucker, such industries accounted for one-quarter of our gross national product by 1955. By 1965, the proportion had grown to one-third and by the late 1970s the percentage of GNP contributed by knowledge industries should pass the half-way mark. Teaching, as a matter of fact, has already become our largest single occupation.

The growth of knowledge industries has been spurred on, and has itself spurred on, the growth of other trends which are making both the people and the situations which Whyte described not only unnecessary but actually dysfunctional. One is the growth of innovation.

At one time, organizations prided themselves on the predictability of their operations, but such predictability is becoming less fashionable and less profitable all the time. An executive of Fairchild Camera Corporation noted in 1967 that "half of the products we will be making in five years don't even exist today." As the rate of change continues to accelerate, organizational conformity becomes less of a help and more of a hindrance to organizational growth or even organizational survival.

This mounting need for innovation is bringing many changes to organizational life. It places priority on men and women who can think for themselves and frowns on those who slavishly seek to imitate their peers and superiors. It requires organizations to blink at or even welcome human eccentricities when such features are part of a human being's package of potentialities. It forces organizations to emphasize internal cooperation and discourage competitiveness. For innovation in the complex technology of today requires teamwork. Competitiveness, which leads to backbiting and mutual sabotage, can spell an organization's death warrant. In short, the modern organization must provide an atmosphere where the imaginative and the gifted can develop and exercise their talents to the utmost.

Another feature that is helping to create the new organization climate is specialization. This, as we have already seen in Chapter II, is bringing down the organizational pyramid and with it the authoritarian approaches which were its main bases of operation. Authority is now coming to rest more and more on expertise, and expertise itself is becoming more and more widely distributed. There are more and more different kinds of experts and they all have their spheres of authority. Furthermore, one man's expertise may be supremely important on one project but may be less vital, though still useful, on another. This helps bring about a circulation of leadership roles as one expert assumes prime responsibility for one undertaking, but defers to another in a different task which requires his expertise somewhat less.

The growth of innovation and specialization is playing havoc with what has been a fairly entrenched feature of bureaucratic personnel management, namely, personnel classifications. Whyte had a good deal to say about personnel classifications and little of what he said was complimentary. It has long been customary for government and big business to devise categories in which to fit and grade their personnel. Under modern conditions, however, such schemes are becoming increasingly outmoded. The need for continually shifting duties and assignments and moving people into and out of leadership roles, and the difficulty of trying to arrange various forms of expertise into a vertical mosaic of grades and ranks, is compelling organizations to make their personnel classifications broader and looser to the point where, in some organizations, they have already started to disappear. The organizational man of Whyte's time who was oriented towards trying to climb a tightly-runged ladder now finds himself rambling on a rather flat plain with fewer and fewer preset guideposts to direct his path.

Accompanying this rapid growth of specialization has been a steady increase in professionalization. In 1945, professionals amounted to only

6.6 percent of the work force. By 1965 they made up 12.3 percent of the work force and they have been climbing rapidly ever since. The number of scientists and engineers rose at a rate that was nearly five times as fast as the population from 1950 to 1965. Such trends have made themselves felt in organizational life in a variety of ways. For example, when the United Auto Workers Union won certification as the bargaining agent at North American Aviation in 1941, it covered some 85 percent of the company's employees. By the early 1960s, the number of employees it was representing at the plant had shrunk to 35 percent.

The trend toward professionalization of the work force shows no sign of easing up. As service industries and automation continue to grow, blue-collar and clerical jobs will continue to decline. It has been estimated that by 1972, at least seven out of ten jobs will require two or more years of college level education.

Professional men do not make good organizational men, at least in William Whyte's use of the term. "They seemingly derive their rewards from inward standards of excellence, from their professional societies, from the intrinsic satisfaction of their tasks," wrote Philip E. Slater and Warren G. Bennis in 1964. "In fact they are committed to the *task*, not the job; to their standards, not their boss. And because they hold degrees, they travel. They are not 'good-company men'; they are uncommitted except to the challenging environments where they can 'play with problems.' " Some five years later, Bennis noted, that now "the good place to work resembles a super-graduate school alive with dialogue and senior colleagues, where the employee will work not only to satisfy organization demands, but, primarily those of his own profession."

Empirical studies are increasingly substantiating these contentions. One example is an investigation undertaken in Great Britain in the mid-1960s to discover the causes of the "brain drain" which was drawing the nation's scientists and engineers to the United States. The survey found that the possibilities of developing or working on new projects was an even greater factor than that of money in inducing professionals to cross the Atlantic.

It should be kept in mind that it is often futile and may even be counterproductive for an organization to try to break the professional's primary commitment to his own profession rather than to the organization itself. If the organization succeeds in doing so, it may only be at the price of rendering the professional incapable of giving the organization what it most needs from him, namely the highest utilization of his talents.

EDUCATION AND ORGANIZATION MAN

From all that has been said regarding the growth of knowledge work in general and the growth of professionalization, specialization, and innovation, in particular, it is apparent that education is playing and will play an ever greater role in organizational life. This is not only true but is more apt to be understated than overstated.

Educational levels are rising and will continue to rise significantly in the coming decades. During the 1960s the number of college students in the United States more than doubled and two-thirds of this increase was due to a rise in the proportion of high school graduates continuing their education. In Germany there was a similar doubling in the number of university applicants during the same decade and the figure was expected to double again by 1980. Japan expects that nearly one-third of all its beginning employees will have a secondary school education by 1972. Other industrial countries report similar progress.

It is sometimes contended that all this education is not really necessary, that people are actually becoming overeducated for their jobs. Those putting forth such an argument frequently cite countries such as Germany and Japan where economic and technological growth has been achieved with what seem to be far lower educational levels than those in the United States. However, this contention can be refuted on two grounds.

For one thing, educational levels are not necessarily lower in Western Europe and Japan even though the average number of years spent in school is less. American education is notoriously easy and lax compared with that of most other developed countries. Western European nations, for example, have a much longer school year and a much more rigorous course schedule. The average American college graduate would have great difficulty passing the university entrance examinations in most European countries. These examinations frequently require translation into and from foreign languages, the solving of problems in calculus, physics, and chemistry, and a near flawless command of the country's own language. A university education in Europe is usually on a level with the best graduate school education in the United States.

As far as Japan goes, its educational process from kindergarten up to and through the university is still more rigorous. Takeo Fukuda, the country's finance minister, claims flatly that Japan has already the highest educational level in the world. While there may be some nationalist pride behind this claim, it is worth noting that Japan already boasts the highest reading rate in the world.

Is all this education necessary? It certainly is. For not only is knowledge work growing, but even those jobs that are not customarily associated with high educational attainment are changing. The National Manpower Council has pointed out that electricians may soon have to learn hydraulics while machinists will have to work with tolerances measured in light waves. Furthermore organizations will increasingly want educated people even for jobs that don't in themselves require extensive schooling. As the rate of innovation continues to accelerate, the organization will need employees who are capable of continually learning new things. An educated employee, no matter what he is doing, will, on the average, have a greater ability to accept and assimilate further training.

Many organizations today are encouraging and even requiring their employees to engage in what at first glance might seem to be a form of educational overkill. For example, Brown-Forman Distillers Corporation, which is scarcely a knowledge industry, makes it almost mandatory for their executives to have at least two college degrees. Several of their management people have Ph.D.'s acquired after they started working for the company. For at least part of the time they received leaves of absence *with* pay in order to obtain them. The company gives two reasons for this policy. The first is that the acquisition of a graduate degree is a sign of motivation. The second, according to president Robbie Brown, is that "a man with a graduate degree by definition is a better-rounded man." And he adds, "we don't care what subject a man gets his graduate degree in." Since the distilling company managed to increase its per-share earnings some 600 percent from 1958 to 1968, no one can claim that its policy has done it any harm.

A by-no-means-unusual advertisement in *The New York Times* sheds further light on this growing need for stepped-up education. The ad reads, "Nationally known corporation with landholdings throughout U.

S. seeks aggressive businessman with degree in city planning, architecture or C.E. Master's degree desirable. Will be responsible for coordinating all aspects of Real Estate and Land Developments. Must be skillful negotiator with exposure in zoning and financial analysis."

Note, if you will, that though the educational requirements call for a degree in city planning, architecture, or civil engineering, the position stipulated is that of a "businessman" who should be "a skillful negotiator." In other words, technical expertise and advanced education are now requirements for roles that were formerly performed by persons whose main professional competence lay in their familiarity with the dollar sign.

We find the same growing emphasis in education in the public sector, although its primary thrust so far has remained largely confined to the federal level. Many universities have added programs is public administration in recent years expressly to cater to part-time government workers. However, graduate degrees in public administration are not the only pathways to progress in the public sector. In almost any federal agency today one comes across executives who acquired or are acquiring graduate degrees in a variety of subjects including history, international relations, and what have you. The thrust is upon acquiring education *qua* education and often no great emphasis is placed on any particular educational track.

The organization which Whyte described and the men who composed it cannot survive this educational upsurge. A report entitled "Our Future Business Environment" which was issued by the General Electric Corporation in 1968 makes this abundantly clear. "Education changes attitudes, particularly the self-image of those who acquire it," said the report. Educated people have more self-respect and demand more respect and treatment as individuals. At the same time, they are less tolerant of authority and organizational restraints. They possess different and higher expectations of what they think a job should provide, the GE study emphasized.*

Education increases the degree of nonconformity in the individual and also increases his tolerance of nonconformity in others. To cite just one of numerous examples of this subject, Samuel A. Stouffer divided a

---

* Those who know General Electric's labor practices may detect an irony here. Like so many other institutions and individuals, the company has often refused to practice what it preaches. GE has long been known for its poor labor relations policies which have caused it to sustain six strikes in 25 years.

sample of 5,000 Americans into three categories: less tolerant, in-between, and more tolerant. He based his evaluations on answers to such questions as whether Communists should have the right to free speech, etc. Only 20 percent of all farmers and 30 percent of all manual workers fell into the more tolerant category. However, over half of all managers, proprietors, and officials, and a full two-thirds of the professional and semiprofessional groups landed in the high tolerance classification.

Another related human attitude which correlates positively with education, and negatively with organizational behavior on the Whyte model, is simple trust. This too has been borne out in a welter of studies which show that educated people display more trust and are more inclined to feel they have close friends than do those who are less schooled. For example, the Louis Harris poll reported on February 25, 1969 the results of a survey it had taken. It had asked respondents the extent to which they believed in this statement: "If you don't watch out for yourself, nobody else will." Among the groups expressing the most agreement with such a statement were blue-collar workers and the least educated. Among the groups expressing least agreement with such a cynical and self-orientated statement were the college educated, business executives, and professionals.

The growth of education provides the main thrust for the administrative revolution. It is producing more and more individuals who are less and less willing to endure, and less and less able to function in, the coercive, conformist, and competitive conditions which characterize the organizations that Whyte so effectively attacked. Combined with the growing need for innovation, specialization, and professionalization, the emergence of educational man is slowly but surely spelling the doom of organization man.

THE SMALL GROUP

The modern organization is coming to place increasing emphasis on the task-force approach to achieving its goals. This has disturbed many who see in it a further demise of the individual and his creativity. Small groups are blamed for stifling initiative and producing bland people and bland ideas. Instead of the wild bursts of imagination which are so often attributable to lonely individuals working independently, we are falling back on what is disdainfully called groupthink. So goes the argument which is frequently voiced regarding the emergence of the small group as the lynchpin in modern organization life. Are the fears and alarms which it reflects justified?

Most probably not. Group decision-making, far from inhibiting creativity, more often stimulates and liberates it. The small group may, and usually does, provide the support and confidence, along with the catalyzing sparks, which allows creativity to blossom. Various studies consistently indicate that people in groups will take greater risks and make better decisions than they would as individuals. The small group reduces responsibility and thereby the feelings of guilt if there is failure. At the same time, it provides the basis for a cross-fertilization of ideas which works for the benefit of all concerned.

MacGregor, an early and ardent advocate of what might be called small groupism, pointed out that frequently we misjudge the potential or actual behavior of such units. In his posthumously published book *The Professional Manager*, he noted that such groups, when properly constituted and utilized, will support and enhance human development.

> Such groups *do* make decisions that are effectively implemented without the necessity for external pressure or surveillance. They are creative and innovative; they operate efficiently; they are not crippled by disagreements or hampered by dominant personalities. Pressures for conformity are minimal and the knowledge and skills of each member are effectively utilized. The outputs of the group are not mediocre, least-common-denominator compromises, but can often yield decisions and problem solutions at a general level of performance superior to the sum of the outputs of the individuals separately. Finally the members perceive the group to be a setting within which there are attractive opportunities to achieve many of their individual goals and to gain intrinsic rewards while *at the same time* contributing to the goals of the organization. (Italics in original.)

The emergence of the small group as a basic unit of the new administration does not portend the end of individual growth and development but rather its furtherance and enhancement. Man is a social animal and, as MacGregor points out elsewhere in his book, there are ample anthropological findings to indicate that his ascendance up the evolutionary ladder is marked by increased feelings of altruism, generosity, and idealism and decreased feelings of hostility and acquisitiveness. The small task-force group provides the device for protecting and nurturing these social qualities for the benefit of all concerned.

One small group which has come into increasing organizational usage in recent years merits some special attention. This is the T group which is the prime device used for what is called sensitivity training. Programs for sensitivity training usually last from two days to two weeks and are designed to allow and encourage the members of the group to act out and express their feelings to one another on a frank and uninhibited basis. They are, or should be, guided by a professional trainer. Over 1,000 business firms and an increasing number of government agencies are now using sensitivity training, and over one-half of the top executives of the country's largest corporations have experienced a human laboratory or T group.

T groups have been bitterly attacked by such organizations as the John Birch Society for supposedly inducing massthink and making robots out of free men. Actually, as is obvious from even the brief description given above, the opposite is the case. Other critics have cited T groups as proof that modern organizations have become so stifling that they must now set up artificial valves which, these critics claim, only allow them to continue in their normal dehumanizing ways. This assumption also fails to ring true. T groups are an expression of modern man's increasing resistance to constricting patterns of behavior that have been with him throughout most of his history. In the words of Warren Bennis, they mark an attempt to create a "counter-culture."

The growing interest of organizations in sensitivity training indicates that they are looking for ways to make this counter-culture more and more part of their normal behavior. Sensitivity training approaches and attitudes are gradually starting to influence organizational life. A recent magazine article indicates this in its title "It's OK to Cry in the Office." Psychology professor Stanley D. Klein of the University of Massachusetts warns that T Groups can be touchy and troublesome. They require leaders who are well-trained and they require participants who have genuinely manifested a desire to participate. But if the proper conditions are met, then, says Klein, "sensitivity training can definitely lead to more sensitive organizations."

CHANGING ORGANIZATIONAL ROLES: THE OUTSIDER

The 1930s were a time of both privation and principle. Idleness flourished but so did idealism. The semiparalysis in which the country's economy lay gripped was a source of despair to some but, in a certain way, a delight to others. If it produced misfortune and misery, it also generated hope and high-mindedness.

Those who fell into the latter category pinned much of their expectations on the American labor movement. This hitherto slumbering sector of American society was suddenly alive with yeasty ferment. Not only was the American Federation of Labor starting to stir but a new labor organization arose which was opening up new horizons for the American worker and the society of which he was a part. This was the C.I.O. which wanted industrial-wide unionism and a welfare state.

This spurt in labor activity produced many new institutions. Among them was the National Labor Relations Board (NLRB). Although designed ostensibly to help both management and labor, its creation was often viewed as a victory for the latter. The NLRB was designed to administer and enforce the new labor legislation, the passage of which was in itself a tribute to the country's burgeoning labor movement. This legislation governed not only relations between management and labor but also relations between the unions themselves.

The NLRB captured the attention and the enthusiasm of many idealists of the time. One of these idealists was Maurice Howard.

In 1934, Howard left his job as an instructor at Reed College to take a position as field examiner with the NLRB Seattle office. His superior at Reed had warmly recommended him for the post and his new superior at the NLRB, Regional Director Charles Hope at first felt the same way. However, by 1936, Hope's attitude towards the former academic began to change.

Hope complained about Howard to Washington, saying that the examiner was getting overly involved in the unions he was charged with overseeing. Howard, said Hope, had frankly stated that he believed the NLRB's function was not to protect labor's right to organize but to help it actually do so. Furthermore, the zealous examiner seemed to show a partiality for the militant C.I.O. unions over the more conservative A.F.L. units. The NLRB sent Howard a reprimand but it was a mild one. Some of the NLRB board members suspected that Hope himself was too partial to the A.F.L. and this was influencing his criticism of Howard.

In addition to cautioning Howard on his behavior the Board also transferred him to the NLRB's Los Angeles office at no loss of salary. Howard took this toned-down disciplinary rebuke good-humoredly, writing back to the Board's chairman, "For me, a former pedagogue who has heretofore been safely sheltered from life's evil ways, to become suddenly identified as a labor factionalist is something which I cannot avoid viewing with mixed emotions. It is so reminiscent of the chaste cleric who, faced with accusations of being a roue, is ashamed to confess his innocence . . . I agree with you that my work need not include the doing of the things I have been represented as doing. They will not be done . . ."

In Los Angeles, Howard soon gained the respect and admiration of his new boss, Towne Nylander. The field examiner's salary was eventually raised to $3,200 a year, quite a tidy sum in those lean and noninflationary times. His career seemed to be progressing smoothly.

But all was not as it seemed. Howard soon began to suspect Nylander of harboring sympathies for the A.F.L. and antipathies for the C.I.O. Nylander himself, it should be emphasized, certainly did much to nurture such suspicions. He had already had trouble with other field examiners over this very point and many of them had left or transferred out of this office. Howard decided to stay on and fight and he had little trouble in winning the adherence of most of the examiners who took the places of his former colleagues. Nylander's persistent attempts to favor the A.F.L., which was in itself favored by business groups over the C.I.O., and Nylander's general handling of the office prompted five of the six examiners to form a clique to stop him. The sixth examiner remained neutral.

Howard emerged at the head of this office cabal. However, it should be kept in mind that though he was zealous, even fanatical about the mission of NLRB, and although he sympathized with labor's left-wing, as represented by the C.I.O. unions, there was no evidence that he slighted or distorted any cases brought in by right-wing A.F.L. unions.

The situation steadily worsened. Nylander's flagrant partisanship and his intemperate speech and behavior in dealing both with the labor movement and his own staff gradually eroded his authority and his prestige. Soon the examiners began trying to obstruct what they felt was the Regional Director's fallacious and possibly corrupt ways of doing things. The examiners even went to the point of hiding information from Nylander and giving him less than full and candid accounts of the work they were doing.

While the Los Angeles field examiners were secreting information from their immediate superior, they were not, however, seeking to hide matters from their Washington headquarters. On the contrary, they sent a letter to the Board's secretary whom they thought would be sympathetic to their position, detailing what they felt were Nylander's shortcomings and abuses. When the Board failed to respond with vigorous corrective action, the field examiners chipped in to buy one of their number an airplane ticket to Washington so that he could talk with the Board members directly and present their evidence. This move also failed to secure requisite action—the Board merely urged Nylander to get along better with the C.I.O. The examiners, meanwhile, were no longer just withholding information from Nylander but were actually leaking certain things to C.I.O. officials. They subsequently explained this as being necessary in order to retain the confidence of the increasingly irate C.I.O. men in the NLRB.

Eventually matters came to a head. A full investigation was launched and Nylander was found to be unsuitable by reasons of temperament and personality for his job of Regional Director. No solid evidence of outright collusion on his part with employers and A.F.L. officials was found and he was permitted to resign. The Board's investigators also recommended transfer for all the field examiners involved with the exception of Howard. As the ringleader of the office cabal, they felt he should be either dismissed or strongly reprimanded and transferred to the East coast on a probationary status.

The adventures and misadventures of Maurice Howard have been written up in a perceptive and even-handed case study by William H. Riker and published as part of the Inter-University Case Studies series entitled *The NLRB Field Examiner*. The case has become a favorite in public administration courses. I, myself, studied it as a graduate student and use it today in teaching both graduate and undergraduate courses. The changing reaction of students to Maurice Howard and the fuss he stirred up sheds light on the changing nature of administration and the way in which it is viewed.

Riker's case study ends with a decision on Howard's future left up in the air. One Board members favors retention with probationary status and transfer; a second member demands dismissal; the deciding vote is up to the chairman. "How do you feel the chairman should have voted?" asks Riker, thus bringing the case to a close in a Lady-or-the-Tiger fashion.

When I was a student, and the instructor polled the class to get a straw vote, almost every member voted to fire. Now I find that when I poll my students, the younger ones, at any rate, usually favor the milder approach by a decisive majority. This changing attitude towards Maurice Howard reflects the changing attitude towards the role of the organizational outsider.

Howard was what is normally called an outsider. He operated outside the usual organizational norms with an independence and a fanaticism which put him at odds with its formalized procedures though, in this instance, not with his co-workers. In the 1930s a man like Howard was anathema to the typical organization; in the 1970s he is becoming more and more of a needed and valued asset.

As a closer examination of the case will show, Maurice Howard's net effect on the NLRB was positive. Though he failed to abide by the rules, though he helped stir up internal trouble and dissension, his efforts in the final analysis benefited the NLRB and probably saved it from much worse trouble in the future. Without his display of unorthodox initiative, the NLRB's Los Angeles office would probably have eventually been confronted with a major scandal. As it turned out a serious problem that was not of Howard's making was discovered and corrected.

Howard's impact was certainly not atypical of the effect of many so-called "outsiders" on the organizations to which they belonged. Such "outsiders" are instruments of correction and change. They thus help supply the organizations of the postindustrial era with what these organizations most need to survive and grow. Howard was above all a zealot, and as Anthony Downs points out in his book *Inside Bureaucracy*, "bureaus with rapidly changing social functions or functions that must be carried out in swiftly shifting environments must strongly encourage zealots" for they are the "idea men who are typically dissatisfied with the *status quo* and are willing to propose new or radical methods." Since the modern organization is becoming ever more compelled to carry out its functions in "swiftly shifting environments," the modern organization needs its Maurice Howards.

The changing nature of the organization is giving wide scope to the men and women it formerly avoided. Whereas such people were formerly shunted to the periphery of the organization, they are now brought into its center. Those with the least obedience to normal organizational restraints are likely to be those on whom the organization depends the most. Boat-rocking is becoming increasingly necessary for an organization to keep itself afloat.

The coddling of organizational members previously regarded as near-outcasts sometimes reaches amazing proportions. This is particularly true of scientists. The problem of the "straying scientist" has become a bothersome one for many organizations. Scientists, it seems, are apt to develop sudden interests in things which have no relationship to what the organization is trying to do. However, it is difficult to discover their wandering until it is too late or even if it isn't, it is still difficult to discourage it. Some management experts have taken to recommending that, as a last resort, the organization allow the scientist to pursue his fancy and, if he comes up with something interesting, the organization should expand its operations to take advantage of it, even though his work may lie completely outside his normal activities. In some cases this would even lead the organization to buying out another company for the express purpose of capitalizing on the straying scientist's discoveries.

Of course, not all outsiders are so productive. There are those who fall into the category of distinct failures. But, here too, organizational attitudes are rapidly changing. Many are devoting increasing energy and resources in trying to salvage such people. For example, at one time the problem drinker received short-shrift from any organization with which he became connected, Now, the trend is to try to rehabilitate him. By the end of 1969 the *Wall Street Journal* estimated that the number of companies with alcoholic rehabilitation programs had reached 1,000. This figure, according to the *Journal*, was some ten times the number of companies sponsoring such programs a decade before.

What has been responsible for this development? One fact is the labor shortage which tends to make any employee more valuable. Another reason is the changing attitudes of management towards misfits. "Many employers hate to fire a worker for what they now view as a disease," said the *Journal*.

For those with whom the organization cannot achieve any *modus vivendi* there is still a good deal more consideration shown than was certainly the case in the past. Instead of firing him outright, the organization tends to induce him to leave of his own accord. It is not unusual for the organization itself to try to place him where he can be happier and more productive. For example, another *Wall Street Journal* survey found that many Wall Street law firms had taken to finding good positions in other firms, "for those employees they decide are not partnership material." In other cases early retirements or consultation contracts are worked out for long-term employees who are no longer considered adequate. Even when it becomes necessary simply to sever all ties, modern organizations are tending to balk at outright dismissals. They are, instead, taking to such methods as giving the failed employee assignments that he doesn't like or no assignments at all in the hope that he will get the message. While scarcely a pleasant experience for any such employee, it does permit him to seek other work while he is still drawing a paycheck and while he still enjoys the "leverage" of being employed in negotiating with prospective employers.

Yes, organizational attitudes towards outsiders and misfits have changed considerably since William Whyte's book burst on the scene. And these changes show every sign of continuing and increasing. They are not, however, confined to rank-and-file organizational members alone. These changes are also affecting directly and drastically those who direct the organization itself.

CHANGING ORGANIZATION ROLES: LEADERSHIP

Gerald G. Frisch reports that during the 1950s a large American aircraft company invited a noted British airplane designer to become its vice-president of engineering. After closely examining what the position entailed, the designer flatly rejected the offer. "I am trained to be an aircraft designer, not an office boy," he said. "Here in America I am shocked to learn that your chief designer is what you call an executive; he shuffles papers, has meetings, approves budgets, interviews senior draftsmen, and so forth. I wouldn't enjoy that at all."

This incident tells us much of the changing nature of leadership in the modern organization, and it is a change that is affecting all kinds of organizations in all kinds of ways. Furthermore, although Great Britain may have been ahead of the United States in the particular industry and position at the time the incident occurred, the change it illustrates has been and is spreading to all technologically advanced countries. In some respects it has made more headway in the United States than in other countries.

The first lesson to be drawn from this episode is that organizational leaders now are turning their backs on administrative work. Their growing professionalism makes them disdain such activity. Furthermore, the organization can usually take better advantage of their gifts by divesting them of such burdens. As a result, administrative duties are being increasingly passed to lower echelon people. This means that administration is more and more being thought of as a service function rather than as a directing function, and it is being carried out more and more by people who have little or no formal authority over those whom they supposedly "administer."

A good example of this is the unit administrator system which many hospitals are adopting. The unit administrator is charged with administering a ward or a floor or some other medical unit. However, he has no authority over the ward or floor nurse, let alone the doctors. His task is rather to relieve such people of their nonprofessional duties so that they can concentrate on doing what they have been trained to do, which is to care for the ill and the injured. The unit administrator's responsibilities are by no means minor. He has to see to it that the ward or floor operates efficiently. However, he has little actual authority to discharge this task. He must rely on his tact and persuasiveness, on diligence and helpfulness if he is to fullfill his obligations.

We find the same basic system at work in many agencies of the federal government. The administrative officer is no longer at or even near the top of the organization. Though he may spend more time than most other senior staff members working with the agency head, he has little formal authority. In the last government agency for which I worked, the administrative officer had a lower rating and drew less pay than any member of the agency except for the secretaries and research assistants. He had great, in some respects, almost crushing responsibilities. Yet he discharged these by exercising an almost infinite amount of patience and persistence and, of course, by working extended hours.

Thus, employees of organizations are being increasingly "administered" by people who tend, if anything, to be their subordinates rather than their superiors. In many situations, the regular employee is more likely to issue orders to the administrator than the other way around. In actual fact, of course, few real orders are issued either way. Thus, one aspect of the administrative revolution is to professionalize administration itself and thereby, in this case, lower its status in the organization.

As the true leaders of the organization tend to shed administrative duties, they take on others which also alter their relationship to their subordinates. Since the modern organization, as we have continually noted, is tending to be staffed increasingly with professional and semi-professional employees, leaders of such employees must make various and often drastic adjustments.

The new organizational leader finds increasingly that he can obtain more from his subordinates by acting as their teacher rather than as their director. He wants them to develop their capabilities to the utmost for on such development the future of the organization may rest. He has less and less need to motivate them to work. They have already invested much time, energy, and money in preparing themselves and are eager rather than loath to utilize their talents. What he has to do is to create the environment and provide the guidance that will allow them to use the abilities which they have worked so hard to acquire. As a matter of fact, the relationship between him and his subordinates is based not so much on what he can tell them to do but on how he can help them do what they already want to do. This changes not only his attitude towards them but also changes their attitudes towards him in some interesting ways.

Two examples illustrate this changing relationship. The supervisor of a small group of social workers informed the agency head that she was resigning. The agency head, having complete confidence in the three case workers whom she was supervising, and wanting to save money, decided to let the case workers work without supervision, at least for the balance of the budgetary year. The case workers, however, felt quite differently. Although they liked and respected the agency director, they informed him, after having talked the matter over among themselves, that unless he hired a new supervisor for them they would leave. They didn't want to handle their more difficult cases without having someone of greater experience to oversee their efforts. In other words, they demanded to have a boss.

Similarly, a young economist was hired by a regional agency with the idea that he would work under a senior member of his profession in the agency's planning department. However, the agency procrastinated in hiring another economist so the young economist finally quit. He was not overworked and he had no bitterness towards the agency itself. He merely felt that he could not learn and develop fully unless he worked under and along with other economists, and so he took a job with a consulting firm where he could do so.

In the professional environment, relationships between superior and subordinate thus undergo a two-way transformation. The superior not only cultivates the goodwill and personal development of a subordinate, but the subordinate looks to the superior as less of a burden to be borne and more as a resource to be utilized.

This new pattern of superior-subordinate relationships diminishes greatly, if it doesn't rule out completely, the exercise of manipulation. If we define manipulation as the process of getting someone to do something without his full knowledge or consent, then it has an increasingly dwindling role to play in modern administrative life. For one thing manipulation becomes less and less necessary. Professionals don't have to be tricked into performing their best. For another thing it becomes increasingly dangerous. MacGregor warned of the hazards of manipulative leadership, pointing out that it can backfire once it is recognized. The employee then becomes suspicious and resentful, and the whole organizational atmosphere becomes poisoned. As the work force becomes more educated and sophisticated, and more protective of its dignity and independence, it will tend to discover manipulation more quickly and react against it more fiercely.

Needless to say, this new pattern of organizational leadership is producing a new breed of organizational leaders. These new leaders are not only more tolerant of nonconformity, but are also more nonconformist themselves. One study of business school graduates showed that those who ranked lowest in conformity tended to be those who turned out to be most successful in their business careers. Another interesting study showed that those members of a business school class who ranked near the top of the class in a test of masculine patterns of interest met with less success in large organizations than those whose interests were more "feminine." "Masculine" interests refer, among other things, to aggressiveness and power-seeking. "Feminine" interests are characterized by more desire for interpersonal relationships, etc.

Thus, a new humanistically-oriented leader is beginning to emerge in organizational life. He is much more deeply and broadly educated than his predecessors. (Levinson notes that already by 1963, close to one-half of all top managers in business had masters degrees and nearly one-fifth had Ph.D's. The number in both categories has risen significantly since then.) He is more ethically oriented than his predecessors. (Raymond Baumhart found that of 1800 business leaders he studied, some four-fifths of them had at one time or another passed up a chance for gain or promotion because it involved unethical behavior.) He also functions more as a democratic leader. (He must negotiate with a wide variety of divergent and frequently conflicting groups such as employees, stockholders, various government agencies, and the public.)

Such men demonstrate areas of interest and concern which differ sharply from those which characterized their forebears of even a few years ago. For example, a poll of business leaders by *Fortune* magazine in September 1969, showed that the second greatest area of agreement among them was this statement: "Business can and should do more about employing the unemployed, and about other social and environmental problems such as supporting education and combating air and water pollution." (Their greatest area of agreement was in recognizing the danger of the Vietnam War to the country's economy.) On specific questions, *Fortune* found that 36 percent of all the business leaders it queried agreed that "business was overly concerned with profits and not enough with public responsibilities," while 46 percent or nearly half agreed with the statement that the "economic well-being in this country is unjustly and unfairly distributed."

There are indications that the incoming crop of business leaders will be even more socially inclined. In May 1970, the faculty and students of Harvard Business School passed a resolution which they publicized in an advertisement in the *Wall Street Journal.* The resolution read as follows:

We condemn the administration of President Nixon for its view of mankind and the American community which:

1. perceives the anxiety and turmoil in our midst as the work of "bums" and "effete snobs";

2. fails to acknowledge that legitimate doubt exists about the ability of black Americans and other depressed groups to obtain justice;

3. is unwilling to move for a transformation of American society in accordance with the goals of maximum fulfillment for each human being and harmony between mankind and nature.

This growing social awareness and sense of social commitment is also found in the public sector. A poll of members of the American Society for Public Administration in 1968 evoked the following pattern of response:

1. Nearly 60 percent felt that public administration at present "worked to the advantages of some segments of society and to the disadvantage of others."

2. Over 40 percent agreed that perpetuation of social injustice and

human misery "makes many of the traditional concerns of public administration seem irrelevant."

3. Approximately 62 percent agreed that administrators "should be concerned with devising organizational forms which enhance the influence of those who possess little or no power in the society."

Examples of these new leaders are emerging all around us. There is Walter Mode, the former college professor who joined the federal government in the 1950s. After holding positions as Regional Commissioner for HEW and Regional Commissioner of Social Security, he was elected president of the American Society of Public Administration for 1971 on a platform calling for more direct involvement by the Society in the problems of the times. There is Alfred J. Marrow, holder of a Ph.D. in psychology, who, in addition to heading one of the country's most flourishing textile companies, has found time to write four books. There is Roger P. Sonnabend who, as president of the Hotel Corporation of America, decided in 1968 to grow a beard, to refuse all invitations to have dinner at clubs for which his Jewish background made him ineligible for membership, and who launched a host of programs designed to recruit and develop managerial talent from minority groups. Said Sonnabend, "I realized how dissatisfied I was with the conforming parts of my life that were not really me."

These new trends in leadership, it should be emphasized, are wholly consistent with what modern organizations increasingly need from their leaders. Columbia University professor and businessman Melvin Ashen points out that the new business environment puts its stress on ideas rather than on resources, and it needs leaders capable of coping with the new forces of technical discovery, new environments, and new social and political institutions. "Executives best prepared to survive this challenge," he says, "may turn out to be those equipped to think like philosophers."

The idea of a philosopher-leader has captured the imagination of thinkers throughout much of human history. Plato dreamed of the philosopher-king and viewed him as the key to the creation of utopia. George Bernard Shaw, in his play *Major Barbara*, has munitions-maker Underschaft tell Greek professor Cusins that until Greek professors become munitions-makers, there will be little chance for society to solve its problems. Albert Camus felt the need for such a combination was urgent. "It is now a question of men of action becoming also men of ideals and poets of industry," he wrote in his notebooks. "It is a question of living one's dreams, of putting them into action. Before, one renounced one's dreams and ideals in order not to lose oneself. One must now neither lose oneself nor renounce one's dreams."

Today, we are seeing the emergence of men who live their dreams. Of men who can produce goods *and* teach Greek, or at least thermophysics, of men who are, in a sense, philosopher-kings. And yet, their emergence has been accompanied by no peal of thunder or streak of lightning. They do not light up the horizon. They do not cause us to gasp and applaud in ecstatic emotion. They speak softly, behave impassively, and often wear glasses, sometimes rimless ones. One would think that the new thinker-doer leader would be more colorful than his predecessors. Instead, he is less so.

The great man of business or politics is, as Philip Slater and Warren Bennis have noted, dying out. Remarkable individuals still bob up but they find they must work continually with countless others in order to make themselves effective. Furthermore, the growth of complex specialization, technology, and organization reduces their power to stand out. Business organizations and government agencies are increasingly basing their growth and dynamism on solid management teams or specialist teams and such teams have no place for "heroes."

Many find this transformation a source of distress. James Reston has bewailed the fact that our society is now becoming a case of the bland leading the bland. The technological age turns out many new products copiously but charisma is not one of them.

However, we should think twice before we mourn the passing of the charismatic leader. Such leadership, we should remember, tends to be just as inflexible as bureaucratic leadership while, at the same time, being much more intolerant and injudicious. It is also by nature unstable. As Weber pointed out, "pure charisma does not recognize any legitimacy other than the one which flows from personal strength proven time and again." Decision-making under charismatic leadership is by rule and fiat. And the basis for such decisions may often be whim, caprice, and idiosyncrasy.

The effect of charismatic leadership on its followers is very much a mixed blessing. True, the charismatic leader may inspire the follower to new heights of achievement. But this is usually accomplished by emotionally, as it were, "filling him up." The follower tends to identify with the leader and thereby fails to achieve his own sense of identity.

He lives and participates somewhat vicariously through his leader and in so doing fails to develop his own emotional and even intellectual resources to the utmost. And when the charismatic leader is no longer around, the follower usually feels empty and bereft until a new charismatic figure appears on the scene to "fill him up" again.

In essence, those who succumb to charismatic leadership are always being led. Their self-development will always fall short of achieving what they otherwise could and should achieve. "Unhappy is the land that needs a hero," Bertolt Brecht says in his play *Galileo*. Unhappy, too, he might have added, is the organization which needs a hero. It is one whose members are unable to fullfill themselves, one in which the individual's self-direction and self-motivation have remained stunted and aborted.

Thus the passing of the charismatic leader should be viewed as a cause for rejoicing rather than for lament. It marks the beginning of a new era when men look to themselves to supply their own human essence. The new leader is the one who creates and maintains the conditions which enable them to do so.

In 1954, a Boston television station, WBZ-TV, won an award for its news coverage of a hurricane. As it so happened, the week the hurricane struck happened to be a week in which the station's news director, Dinny Whitmarsh, was on vacation. Thus, when the award was announced, Whitmarsh came in for a lot of good-natured ribbing, the thrust of which was that this showed how dispensable he was. Whitmarsh, however, remained completely unruffled and imperturbed. He calmly pointed out that the ability of his news department to function so well in his absence proved, on the contrary, just what a good news director he was.

The Whitmarsh style of leadership will come increasingly into play in the modern organization. Resting as it does, dependent as it is, on the achievements of professionals and specialists, it will increasingly take to the type of leadership which is somewhat invisible and diffuse. Confucius once said that the right to govern depended on the leader's ability to make the governed happy. The modern organization leader must take this notion to heart, but he must add to it a further precept from Lao-tzu. This latter Chinese sage once pointed out that "when the best leader's work is done, the people say 'we did it ourselves.' "

5

PLANNED FREEDOM

Anyone drawing up a list of bureaucracy's greatest evils would undoubtedly put inertia and routinization somewhere near the top. Next to its tendency toward procrastination and delay, probably no more frequent charge has been flung at the bureaucratic operational method than its tendency to march, or rather crawl, along well-trodden ways, looking neither to the right nor the left, making no provision for what may lie up ahead, and, once encountering the unforeseen, making no significant adjustments to deal with it. "Nobody can be at the same time a correct bureaucrat and an innovator," the economist Ludwig von Mises once scathingly remarked. "Progress is precisely that which the rules and regulations did not foresee; it is necessarily outside the field of bureaucratic activities."

Like most indictments that have been handed down by antibureaucrats against their *bête noire*, this one is overstated and overdrawn. But also, like too many such indictments, it contains an all-too-recognizable element of truth. The bureaucratic style is scarcely an inducement to, or a facilitator of, the new and untried. And the continual testing and adoption of the new and the untried is what the administrative revolution is all about.

The modern organization finds itself confronted with a never-ending challenge to form and reform its structure and its operations, to take on the new and abandon the old, to do today what it did not do yesterday, while, at the same time, getting ready to do still something else tomorrow. Consequently, it must build into its very structure a mechanism for metamorphosis. This mechanism is called planning.

Planning has been described as a way of stabilizing change. The planners peer into the future, try to see what change will be needed, and seek to prepare their organization to meet it. But planning not only stands for change; it also stands for improvement. When an organization adopts planning, it is saying to itself, and to the world, that it realizes that the future will not only be different but that it can also be better.

Large American business corporations were among the first organizations to undertake systematic, long-range planning. Today public agencies are increasingly following suit. Planning officers are cropping up in more and more public agencies both here and abroad. One of the recommendations of the Fulton Commission Report in Great Britain was the establishment of a planning unit in each government department. Entire societies are also making blueprints for their futures. These include cities, states, and even whole countries.

When it comes to planning for an entire nation, however, vast discrepancies exist. Such countries as Japan, France, Sweden and, in a somewhat more disguised fashion, Germany have enthusiastically and successfully taken to the planning process. Britain and the United States, however, still continue to dawdle along the planning path.

The United States in particular has lagged behind in this aspect of the administrative revolution because government planning for the national economy has long been viewed as a manifestation of creeping socialism and all its attendant horrors. In 1963, American businessmen effectively sabotaged an attempt by the Kennedy administration to gather information on business prospects. The businessmen did so because they feared that such information could be used for planning purposes. However, by the end of the decade, American business seemed to be undergoing a change of mind and heart. The havoc which the Vietnam war was causing to the American economy was prompting many business leaders to look for some way of stabilizing the future. Early in 1970, Thomas J. Watson, Jr., president of IBM, called on government to undertake certain planning functions. "The national goals of this country should be set and restudied annually," said Watson as he called for a new governmental body "to sit permanently on this matter and report to the President."

Planning, in its essentials, is the same whether it is for an organization or for a society. (Societies are, in many respects, organizations.) It does not have to have any particular political orientation. Although usually associated with the left, it has often been encouraged and fostered by the right. One of the great planning documents of all times is Alexander Hamilton's brilliant *Report on Manufactures*. French businessmen accepted planning after World War II only to escape nationalization, but they have since become their country's most enthusiastic backers of *le planification francaise*. So have their colleagues in Japan, Sweden, and elsewhere. The planned society, it may be said, is a natural outgrowth of the planned organization for the organization cannot successfully map its own future unless it knows in advance what the environment it will be operating in will be like.

Planning, whether by organizations or by entire governments, has many exciting implications. First, it contributes to dehierarchicalization for it tends to shift the most basic decision-making in organizations out of the hands of its top men. Under planning, staff experts and, as we shall soon see, the entire organization come to play an increasing role in determining the organization's policy. This tends to increase equality and equity within the organization. The inauguration of planning enables small or less powerful units within an organization or a society to become less dependent on the political skill or influence of their leaders. The systematic methods of decision-making which planning encourages permit these subunits to make themselves heard or have their interests taken into account without raising their voices or waging intra-organizational warfare. Those interests in an organization or a community which previously may have been by-passed when it came to deciding who gets what, when, and how are more apt to gain increased consideration when a systematic planning process is underway.

The setting of goals which forms so vital a part of the planning process also increases organizational democracy. Through formalizing the goal-setting process, planning makes decision-making operate within a less arbitrary framework and a more visible arena. This makes it somewhat more difficult, though by no means impossible, for vested interests in a community or favored departments in an organization to obtain special privileges or protection. A company manager may have for years been favoring through extra funds or personnel one branch of the firm which is managed by the man he plays golf with on Sunday. Once the organization starts to plan, the company head may find it harder to do so. Similarly, a city or state may have systematically ignored one pocket of its population. But when it assigns professional planners to draw up a comprehensive plan for its future, and when the plan is made public, the omission of this segment of the community becomes much more glaring and, consequently, more amenable to correction.

This brings us to a related aspect of planning: increased accountability. Employees, stockholders, clients, the press, and the public can more easily evaluate administrative performance when an organization or a society formulates explicit plans and seeks to execute them. Planning not only encourages organizations and societies to make more rational and more equitable choices for the future, but also generates pressure on them to adhere to such choices once they are made.

What about participation? Planning is usually thought of as something which casts a constricting net over the entire organization. Individual initiative and spontaneity is seemingly curtailed for plans, to be successful, must be implemented. However, once again, things are not always what they seem. Planning, or at least successful planning, actually tends to promote rather than impede participation in decision-making.

Planning, above all, requires information. The planners cannot possibly map desirable, let alone realizable goals, without an abundance of data of various kinds. The search for information usually takes the planners into every branch of the organization or every sector of the community. They not only need hard data but soft data as well. They must know the ideas and suggestions of those closest to every significant aspect of the organization's or community's operations. Even when the planners try to omit this latter element from their information search, they usually find it thrust upon them since the quest for information arouses the interest, if not the fears, of the subunits or subcommunities and spurs them to take action. City planning, for example, often seems to incite a tidal wave of discontent but this is often a healthy phenomenon. Those most likely to react with frenzied fury to the planners' schemes are often those who in the past have sat out the process of change on the sidelines. Planning frequently jars them out of their apathy or lethargy and brings them in as participants, albeit hostile ones, to the process of change. Even our early, and therefore, worst urban renewal projects frequently had this salutary effect. In their failure to consult with those in the areas being renewed, the renewers still goaded those affected to mobilize and to become involved. This sometimes reached the point where a sense of community arose within the project area where no such community feeling previously existed.

However, planning needs participation for more than just the purpose of information. The successful implementation of plans usually requires a degree of agreement and concord which participation can best provide. There are usually all sorts of ways in which a community group or an organizational subunit can frustrate or at least seriously impede a section of the plan, and this can frequently lead to the defeat of the entire plan. A plan, we should remember, aims at being a coherent blueprint consisting of interrelated and interdependent parts. It is thus necessary for all its parts to be implemented if the plan itself is to be achieved. Any blockage to any significant portion of the plan may spell doom for all of it.

For reasons such as these, successful planning almost always is accompanied by increased participation. This certainly has been true in France where, apart from government personnel, representatives of some 3,000 organizations now take part in formulating the country's future. True, many others still remain outside the planning process in France, but this in most cases is the reflection of their own wishes and weaknesses. The communist trade unions, for example, still insist that planning is a capitalist trick and refuse to join in its procedures. However, even they are showing signs of coming to terms with this detested device. During the mid-1960s, the communist French unions began sending representatives as observers to the meetings of the various planning commissions. New administrative reforms in Japan during the late 1960s increased the role of planning and, at the same time, increased the role of line and field departments in decision-making. For example, in drawing up the new plan, the central government sent a questionnaire to prefectural and municipal governments eliciting their ideas and attitudes as to what needed to be done.

In Great Britain, the Skeffington report entitled *People and Planning* claimed that many of the failures of planning in the country stemmed from the fact that the public was not adequately informed as to what was being done until it was too late. The report called for community forums to involve as well as inform the public in and about planning. Such a step was deemed necessary to make planning work.

New York City mayor John Lindsay, in his book, *The City*, points to several examples of where planning without consultation with, and participation of, those affected misfired in the United States. The Federal Highway, Public Housing, and early Urban Renewal programs, he notes, often created more problems than they solved. Federal highway programs generated more urban traffic congestion than they alleviated and federal housing programs often weakened rather than strengthened community development. "In essence, after four years as mayor, my belief is this: we cannot plan for the citizenry unless we plan with them . . ."

A Canadian official expresses a similar view. According to M. Brownstone, a staff member of the Royal Commission on Bi-lingualism and Bi-culturalism, "development schemes for situations when devoid of a strong element of local participation and responsibility, have a history of failure." Canada has developed a system of participation called *animation social* and has used it with great success in many regional planning projects.

The concept of planning through participation and consensus takes us to the role of cooperation. By its very nature, planning, to be successful, must expand the level of cooperation and diminish the area of competition in any organization or in any community in which planning is done. Planning can never score any noteworthy victories in a setting of conflict. When the diverse members of groups in an organization or a society are jousting for power and waging internecine warfare, the planners had better watch out. Such activity may not only spell the death of any comprehensive plan but may also seal the doom of the organization or the community itself. The growth of planning has to mean the growth of cooperation. It is not possible for one to flourish successfully without the other.

This need for cooperation usually brings forth further pressure for equality. We have already seen how formalized goal setting and formalized goal implementation tend to reduce arbitrary discrepancies. The compelling need for all sectors and branches to work together only aids and abets this trend. If the various units in the organization or the community suffers from wide disparities in their respective resources and in status, then the have-nots will be too eager to take from the haves to make planning work. Labor and management, as we have seen, cannot effectively plan for a bigger pie unless both sides are reasonably contented with, or at least accepting of, the pattern whereby the slices will be distributed. So it is with any organization and community.

One further implication of planning remains to be examined, and this is the most important implication of all: the effect of planning on human freedom. At first glance it would seem that the citizen of the planned society or the member of the planned organization must forego a certain amount of liberty. Unless a plan can see to it that certain things happen and certain other things don't happen, plans will remain only dreams and hopes. For plans to be realized, the individual must agree to abide by their dictates and surrender some of his discretion. The part must be sacrificed to the whole.

While there is certainly some truth to this contention, its popularity, however, exceeds its validity. First, planning, as we have already seen, requires a good deal of consent. This means that on balance any individual or unit is more likely to gain more of what he or it wants, than he or it is likely to lose what he or it has. An increased ability to share in, and reap the fruit of, the creation of the future is certainly consistent with the expansion of human freedom. To the extent, then, that planning allows this, it broadens rather than narrows the scope of human liberty.

However, there is a further aspect to the planning-freedom relationship which merits careful consideration. The French social scientist Claude Gruson perceptively points out that the planned society allows the individual to choose his own future more intelligently and more securely for he now knows just what is going to happen. In the unplanned society he is left too much to the mercy and caprice of circumstance. He cannot make meaningful choices for he does not know what the future will bring. By reducing uncertainty in societies' or organizations' future, planning actually increases the individual's options, or, to put it another way, make those options more translatable into achieveable goals.

Planning, in short, helps to shield societies, organizations, and individuals from the capricious and the unknown. Instead of being the victims of change, they can now become its masters. Rather than just react, they may now control. And those who feel they have insufficient control or at least are not able to see their own aspirations realized will still have more meaningful control over their own lives for now they know what is coming and can make their own plans accordingly. Thus, the growth of planning is consistent with, and conducive to, the growth of human freedom.

PPBS: THE BUDGETING OF PLANNING

During the late 1950s, British planners watched in dismay and anguish as downtown London became increasingly choked with automobiles. The planners desperately wanted to build a new subway line across the heart of the city to relieve the burgeoning congestion. But they were stymied in doing so. The engineering was available and, potentially, so were the funds. The only trouble was that the financial justification was lacking. No matter how often they sat down with their slide rules to figure things out, the new subway line always came up on the liability side of the ledger. It could not be shown to pay its way and so the authorities continually rejected the idea.

In the early 1960s, however, someone hit upon a new approach. Why not tabulate the savings in travel-time and motor-vehicle operating costs that would result to those who would *not* use the line but who would benefit from the reduced street congestion that the line's construction would produce. When these additional benefits were calculated and figured in, the equation changed drastically. Whereas before the line was slated to be a financial loser, it now came out yielding a return of about 11 percent on the investment required and this yield was after allowing for interest charges on the money that would be borrowed to finance it. Jubilantly the planners presented their new set of calculations to the London authorities. The money was voted and the line was built.

In Boston, Massachusetts, meanwhile, the city's Finance Commission was also pondering the problem of urban transportation and its many financial aspects. Specifically, the commission was giving some hardnosed consideration to the city's municipal parking garage program. Like many American cities, Boston had responded to the postwar upsurge in car travel by building parking garages. The city had constructed some seven such garages and prided itself on its wisdom and foresight in having done so. Periodically, the city government would announce that the garages were returning in revenue from leases more than enough to pay off the cost of their construction. They were also obviously housing numerous cars that would otherwise be on the streets. Ergo, the garage program was a success.

But was it? Boston's Finance Commission was not so sure. With some help from Harvard economist Otto Eckstein, the commission decided to subject the municipal garage program to some searching scrutiny.

The city was correct in claiming that the garages were paying off the cost of their construction, the commission found, but this did not mean that the program was paying for itself. There were other costs which, through inadvertence, perhaps, rather than design, had been left out of the city's press releases. First, there was the cost in terms of foregone tax revenue. The garages had, for the most part, replaced taxable property which would have otherwise gone on producing income for the tax-starved metropolis. This was now lost and had to be accounted for.

Then there was a loss to the city's transit system. Like most such systems, Boston's public transportation was running at a heavy deficit and two-thirds of this deficit had to be paid for by the city itself. The commission polled users of the garage and established a figure of how many of these users would utilize the transit system if the garages were not in existence. These lost transit fares were entered on the debit side of the garage program ledger. When the commission was through with these and other complex tabulations, it found that the program, far from being a financial bonanza, was costing the city over a half-million dollars a year.

However, the program was not originally designed simply to make money. It was also supposed to attract business for the downtown business district. The commission, again using its poll of garage users and securing some informal estimates of shoppers' spending, found the program still wanting. The number of shoppers that the garages were bringing into the city was so minimal that it would have been cheaper for the city to pay the merchants out of its own pocket all the additional profit which the garages were generating for them.

These efforts by the Boston Finance Commission and the city of London in the early 1960s were rudimentary attempts to make use of more sophisticated techniques for figuring public expenditures. These techniques are part of a new system of budgeting called The Planned Program Budgeting System or PPBS.

PPBS made its debut in the public sector during the 1940s. Its first application was in water resource development. Planners, economists, and engineers began making systematic calculations of all the costs and all the benefits involved in various water resource projects to determine their relative attractiveness. PPBS is essentially a method of evaluating alternative ways of achieving goals and it worked well.

Robert McNamara brought PPBS into the Defense Department in the 1960s, and through its use was able to achieve significant economies in the department's vast operations. In 1965, President Johnson directed all federal agencies to make a start at utilizing these new methods in formulating their budgets and PPBS has, in fits and starts, moved forward ever since. A growing number of state and local governments are also beginning to get their feet wet in this new, somewhat chilling, but yet bracing systems stream.

PPBS is a budgetary mechanism designed and engineered for planning. Conventional budgeting, with its emphasis on simply listing objects of expenditure—so many cars purchased and maintained, so many employees hired and compensated—tends to foster an essentially static operation. Traditional budgeting often, indeed usually, has overlooked the desirability and utility of basic programs. It tends to center its attention on simply incremental increases or decreases in what has gone on previously. Each year's budget usually replicates last year's budget, give or take a few expenditure items. And there is little planning beyond the current budget year.

PPBS is designed to change all this. It focuses not on separate items of expenditure but on whole programs. And it subjects these programs to ruthless or at least rigorous analysis. Such analysis seeks to take into account *all* the costs including social and external costs, and *all* the benefits, including social and external benefits. Under PPBS budgeting becomes not just a catalogue of expenditures, but a statement of goals with an evaluation of the various alternatives for their achievement. It is a budgeting system geared not only to planning but also to change and innovation for PPBS facilitates the adoption of the new and the elimination of the old.

PPBS does not, as Professor Bertram M. Gross points out, replace human judgment. Nor does it by itself decide the relative emphasis on major areas of activity such as education versus health, etc. But it does make planners deal with the fact that resources are always finite and relatively scarce, and it makes budgeters more conscious of the aims and purposes of public spending. In other words, to the extent that PPBS does its job, it makes the visionary sector of administration, namely planning, more realistic and the realistic sector of administration, namely budgeting, more visionary.

Because of PPBS's association with Robert McNamara's reign at the Defense Department, it has come to be associated in the minds of some with defense expenditure. And since defense spending is often associated, not without some justification, with evil, PPBS has acquired in some areas a darkly malevolent connotation. However, even if guilt by association were a correct method of evaluating its role, this would not bring PPBS under indictment. McNamara's PPBS techniques were often bitterly opposed by the generals and admirals in the Pentagon. They saw in its application a loss of many pet projects and, more importantly, a loss of much of their discretionary power.

PPBS has found some of its most ardent enthusiasts within the federal agency that is most directly concerned with developing human resources, the Department of Health, Education and Welfare. One HEW study examined through the use of PPBS eight alternative methods of reducing motor vehicle injury. The study showed that the cheapest way of realizing this desirable goal was a seat-belt program. According to the HEW's calculations such a program would cost only $87 for each death averted. The most expensive of the alternatives was a nation-wide driver training program. The HEW budgeters estimated that this method would cost $88,000 for each death averted or more than 1,000 times as much for the same unit of benefit. Such are the workings, and such are the possible benefits, of PPBS.

The HEW program study illustrates still another aspect of the PPBS technique. Next to driver training, the second most expensive method of reducing motor vehicle injury, according to HEW's figures, were grants for establishing medical services. Yet, though such a method would cost $45,000 per death averted, this program was deemed deserving of some HEW support. Why? Because the medical services it would establish would provide health benefits beyond the reduction of vehicle injuries alone. This points to another important feature of PPBS: it takes into account benefits beyond those accruing from the specific goals which a program is designed to achieve.

Like most components of the administrative revolution, PPBS has not had an easy time of it. The new budgeting system has encountered steep slopes and rocky terrain in its march of conquest through the battlegrounds of bureaucracy. Critics have lain in wait at every turn in the road and, to be sure, many of the barbs and arrows they have slung have found their mark.

David Barkley, professor of public administration at Northeastern University, points out some of PPBS's limitations. How, he asks, could you apply its cost benefit technique to the conduct of foreign policy? Certainly, it would be difficult to do so, although some aspects of foreign policy, such as foreign aid programs, could perhaps benefit from more rigorous analysis. PPBS has often been accused of oversimplification and this too has some validity. There is no gainsaying the fact that even in those spheres where it is supposed to work, it has sometimes produced more nonsense than sense.

One PPBS fiasco which critics often point to, and which defenders shamefacedly concede, was an HEW study on motorcycle injuries. The department wanted to reduce the high injury rates which characterize motorcycling in this country. After going through what they thought were all the accepted PPBS rituals, the analysts came up with a proposal for spending $1.7 million over five years in an advertising and public relations program to promote the wearing of motorcycle helmets. How did they arrive at this solution?

They took a study from a foreign country which showed a substantial reduction in mortality and morbidity rates when such a helmet-wearing program was implemented. They decided that a similar reduction would almost automatically be the result in the United States as well. Then they decided that a public relations and advertising program to promote helmet wearing would be 20 percent effective in the first year and increase to 55 percent effectiveness in the fifth year. How they arrived at these figures for gauging the effectiveness of such a publicity campaign is not fully known. Then, basing their calculations on the growth of motorcycle registrations, they decided that this program would save 4,006 lives during its five-year span. (The use of such a precise figure in itself drew a great deal of critical scorn.) This worked out to a cost of $180 per death averted, seemingly a veritable budgetary bonanza. However, the PPBS'ers didn't stop there. They made estimates of the life earnings that the prospective accident victims would now enjoy thanks to the program's efforts in persuading them to wear helmets. After computing these life earnings estimates, the analysts came up with a cost-benefit ratio of 55 to 1.

The study was obviously loaded with faulty or at least fuzzy analysis and became celebrated as an example of the pitfalls and perils of PPBS. Fortunately, Congress saved the situation by eliminating the need for any such program. The lawmakers passed legislation which cut off federal highway funds to any state that did not itself have a law requiring motorcyclists to wear helmets.

But though PPBS has its limitations and its problems, it also has its potentialities. And although some of the criticisms that have been leveled at it are valid, a good many are not.

Some charge that PPBS removes the human element from decision-making. Policy formulation under PPBS, they claim, becomes reduced to a mechanical, robot-like activity. However, the reverse is actually true. Traditional budgeting is much more mechanical and much more limiting on policy-making than is PPBS. As Allen Schick points out, "Program budgeting departs from simple engineering models in which the objective is fixed and the quantity of inputs and outputs is adjusted to an optimal relationship. In PPBS, the *objective itself is variable*;

analysis may lead to a new statement of objectives." (My emphasis.)

Some further examples from HEW will illustrate this point. The Department assessed programs for improving the effectiveness of detecting and treating cancer at four different sites: uterine cervix, breast, head and neck, and colon-rectum. It found that a colon-rectum detection and treatment program would cost $43,000 for each death averted compared to a cost of only $3,500 per death averted in a uterine-cervix program. However, this did not cause HEW to abandon all interest in the detection and treatment of colon-rectum cancer. Instead it called for improved technology in this area.

A study by Werner Z. Hirsch and Morton J. Marcus in the field of education sheds further light on the wide-ranging ramifications and implifications of PPBS. These researchers found that the cost-benefit ratio in junior college education was not as great as had been thought. For males, the benefit ratio ranged from 91¢ to $1.95 for each dollar invested. For females, it fell consistently below a dollar for each dollar expended. But this did not lead the authors to call for the phasing out of junior college education, or the limiting of such schooling to males. Looking at the problem still further, they found that a year of junior college education given through summer work during high school years would produce a benefit-cost ratio ranging up to 3.24 to 1 for males and 1.47 to 1 for females. They therefore suggested that the federal government reconsider whether it should provide up to $3 billion annually for junior colleges if less expensive alternatives were available.

But supposing the researchers had limited their investigations to just junior college evaluations. Would this have led them to recommend that such colleges become all-male institutions? This is hardly likely. First, they would probably not have limited themselves in such a fashion in the first place, for PPBS, we should remember, is the evaluation of alternatives and almost invariably it involves the weighing and comparing of different programs. However, even if their study were so limited, it could still yield various recommendations. Since, presumably, the lower cost-benefit ratio for girls results from their early withdrawal from the work force through marriage and from the lower salaries they earn if they do keep working, one proposal which could easily emerge from such a study would be expanded day center programs for children and equal salaries for women. The analysis provides no more ammunition to antifeminists than it does to women liberationists!

Many foes of PPBS have pointed to the difficulties of putting price tags on things like pain and suffering, to say nothing on human life itself. But these difficulties do not render such approaches impossible or invalid. PPBS, it must be emphasized still once again, primarily examines alternatives. Thus it does not judge a program in terms of dollars and cents so much as it uses dollars and cents to compare one program with another in the attempt to reach a goal. The more lives saved for a given amount of money, the more efficient the program is likely to be even if other measuring sticks than financial ones were to be utilized.

This brings us to another and closely related aspect of PPBS which has aroused the ire and fear of many. These critics concede that cost benefits may be calculable on a dollar and cents basis but they shudder at the very idea of doing so. In their eyes, PPBS is a heartless, techno-logical device that substitutes considerations of machine-like efficiency for the warmth and humanity which should govern the operations of government in any civilized society.

From what has already been said, it should be apparent that this is simply not the case. First, because PPBS does not, as we have seen, establish goals but only provides ways of taking more rational steps towards achieving such goals as are established. Second, because human costs and human benefits almost inevitably turn up as financial costs and financial benefits. Third, because PPBS concentrates not on the operations of public agencies *per se* but on the delivery of public services.

This last-cited point is a cardinal one that merits further examina-tion. All too often in government we tend to judge efficiency apart from actual results. This is sometimes known as the-operation-was-a-success-but-the-patient-died syndrome. The utilization of PPBS tends to curtail if not eliminate such faulty thinking. PPBS focuses intently on the *consequences* of administrative activity. It is not how the operation was performed but what happened to the patient that now assumes top priority. PPBS happily undermines the smug satisfaction in which ad-ministrators have sometimes indulged as they watch a pet program operate smoothly but yield little in the way of tangible social benefits. Under PPBS, criteria of *effectiveness* replace criteria of *efficiency*.

In establishing criteria of effectiveness, PPBS takes into account ex-ternal costs and external benefits. This too tends to emphasize rather than understate human factors. On the cost side much highway con-struction would have been deterred, and greater efforts at water and air pollution control would have been spurred, had PPBS been in wide use in American government over the past 20 years. The true costs of highway building and of water and air pollution were never fully assessed or expressed through previous budgeting methods. On the other side of the ledger, many health, education, welfare, and urban construction programs would have received greater impetus since such activities usually yield important spillover as well as direct benefits—an area PPBS is more apt to assess fully.

PPBS also has a positive role to play in conflict resolution. Its use tends to dampen the personalized bitterness and discord which can prove so damaging and even fatal to democratic values and to democratic society itself. PPBS certainly does not abolish disputes, but it does tend to move conflict to a more depersonalized and intellectual level. The new budgeting technique forces advocates and opponents to spend more time marshalling facts and probing rationales and less time wheeling and dealing or engaging in demagoguery or bombast. Under PPBS, political clout becomes less of a factor in determining budget priorities.

Finally, for all the complicated mathematics which it sometimes uses, PPBS facilitates rather than impairs administrative accountability. Conventional budgets, with their interminable lists of expenditure items, may seem less complicated but they are also much less explicit. All too often, they leave legislators and other scrutinizers completely in the dark as to what is really going on. Such budgets frequently fail to give adequate clues as to just what will happen if any of the budget's items are increased or cut. The legislature, the press, and the public are frequently stymied in their efforts at finding out just what is being done and just what should be done to change what is being done.

PPBS tends to lift the budgetary veil on administrative activity. Now, those who have an interest in supervising or watching over administrative operations can better gauge the effectiveness and efficiency of such operations. The watchers can more easily encourage the adoption or extension of some programs and discourage the adoption or continuation of others.

Despite this fact, legislative bodies, it must be said, do not always take kindly to the introduction of such modern budgeting methods. They tend to cling to the tried and true despite the fact that, in this case, the tried and true has only encouraged the slide into impotence and futility which so many legislatures have experienced in the modern administrative state. However, where PPBS has actually been adopted and used, it has, more often than not, elicited legislative approval and even support. This has been the case in Hawaii and Wisconsin, the only two states now making extended use of PPBS. In Wisconsin, the chairman of the legislature's joint budget committee published a magazine article enthusiastically endorsing PPBS after its first year of use.

PPBS is no miracle method. It does not offer quick and easy solutions to the problems that beset and besiege modern governments and the societies they serve. It remains somewhat primitive in many respects, and, like the administrative revolution of which it is a part, will probably never completely live up to the dreams and hopes of its early supporters. But as its use grows and expands, it will tend to make administration more effective, more responsible, and more responsive to the fulfillment of human needs in modern society.

CENTRALIZATION

Few elements of administration are suffering such massive unpopularity these days as is centralization. As an aspect of the bureaucratic style, centralization is held responsible for causing or aggravating a wide variety of woes. Inflexibility, unresponsiveness, delay, alienation, and even oppression are laid at its doorstep. This marks a radical departure from previous thinking for it wasn't so long that centralization frequently won plaudits and stirred enthusiasm. It was hailed for its efficiency, its smoothness, and its impartiality. But now all that has changed. Centralization to many at present represents the dead hand of bureaucracy at work stifling the human spirit. According to the tenet of much modern thinking, to centralize is to tyrannize; to decentralize is to liberate.

To a great extent, the administrative revolution shares these attitudes. It marks a revolt against inflexibility, unresponsiveness, and directive control. In putting maximum decision-making power in the hands of those nearest the area of action, it pulls power away from the center. Theory Y, it would seem, stands for decentralization or it stands for nothing at all.

But now a problem seems to arise. If we take a second look at PPBS and long-term planning, we note an apparent antithesis. Both seem to have a built-in centralizing bias. How is it possible for the individual and the subunits of an organization "to do their own thing" when the organization is exercising increasing responsibility over its goals, plans, and programs? How does one reconcile PPBS and planning with the decentralizing nature of the administrative revolution?

Other forces currently at work in administration and in society would also seem to make decentralization increasingly difficult, if not impossible. There is, for example, the tendency towards large-scale organization in both business and government. There is the increasing use of computers and other high technology equipment. Such equipment makes it easier for the center to control subunits while it makes the subunits more dependent on the center for information and other resources. The onward march of progress would seem to relegate decentralization to the world of dreams and illusions.

Fortunately, things are again not always what they seem. And, for that matter, neither is centralization itself what it often seems. Let us start by taking a closer and longer look at the whole issue.

Centralization is one of the oldest of administrative problems. Early Near and Far Eastern literature indicate that the task of controlling field officers continually vexed and harassed the emperors and pharaohs of ancient times. However, when we probe a little deeper, we are inclined to give these rulers some sympathy for there was often less oppression of the citizenry when they could exercise control than they could not. The emperor's or the pharaoh's law was often harsh and his taxes were often exacting. But the free-wheeling activities of provisional chieftains were frequently much more burdensome and brutalizing to the common man. And when these local officials could rule independently, there was usually more oppression than when they remained under central control. The misery and brutality which so distressed Confucius took place in a disunited China with a weak puppet king who could not curb the appetites and actions of his ruthless feudal lords.

If we pursue the thread of history up to modern times we find examples of the same pattern continually recurring. Closeness to the scene may foster sensitivity and responsiveness but all too often it does the opposite. Centralization, on the other hand, while it makes for delay and inflexibility, also encourages impartiality and a certain degree of fairness.

The Norman conquerors of England during the Middle Ages, to take one example, ruthlessly centralized such government operations as then existed, and brought the country's feudal lords under central control. At the same time, they instituted the custom of "haro" whereby a subject could appeal to the conscience of the king from an arbitrary action taken against him by his local lord. Such an appeal was launched by simply crying out the word "haro" in the king's presence. William the Conqueror's own funeral was held up by an obscure person named Asselin who broke from the crowd, cried "haro" and claimed that the land in which the king was being buried had been wrongly taken from him by his local duke. Asselin was awarded compensation on the spot. According to Adolph A. Berle, Jr., the conscience-of-the-king procedure became the basis for the British common law court of equity.

Americans these days tend to look back with sighing nostalgia to a time when political institutions seemed more decentralized. They forget that was also a time when Negroes were lynched, dissenters were deprived of basic rights, and paupers were either subject to the whim of political bosses or shut up in poor farms. Rectification or at least amelioration of these and a host of other abuses have come about primarily through the intervention of higher levels of authority.

Studies by political scientists also shed light on this issue. They show that the smaller the constituency, the more likely it is to be under the control of an elite. Small town America, to any one who has examined it closely, shows much more discrimination, much more arbitrariness, and much more favoritism than does big city America. The same trend has been seen in other lands as well. One reason why the British, the Swedes, and the Germans have been abolishing their municipal police forces is that such forces have shown too much susceptibility to local power pressures at the expense of impartiality and fairness.

The larger the governmental unit, James Madison wisely noted, the more likelihood there was that it would take in a variety of what he called "factions." As a result, the less likelihood there would be for any particular faction to dominate. Furthermore, the larger the unit, the more visible it would be and the more attention it would evoke. This too tends to act as a curb on capricious or injudicious behavior. Finally, the larger the unit, the more it would be forced to standardize its activities. In so doing, it tends to narrow the possibilities for personal arbitrariness and personal abuse.

This is as true for business as it is for government. As a boy, I remember seeing the owner of a small hardware store mercilessly berate and humiliate his middle-aged salesclerk while customers stood around and rather uncomfortably watched. Such behavior is almost unthinkable today. This is due in part to the fact that jobs are no longer so scarce and employees are less dependent on employers. It is also partly due to the trend toward large-scale organization with its depersonalized methods of handling personnel. We rail against such depersonalization today, and in a sense, it is right that we should. But the man I saw being subjected to some highly personal treatment from a small proprietor would have welcomed what we now decry.

Thus, centralization, like the mask of Thespis, has both a grim and benign face. It does tend to promote inflexibility, insensitivity to local or particular needs, and procrastination and delay. But it also helps to insure impartiality and equality. It tends to protect its employees and clients from arbitrary actions by local superiors and power holders, but at the same time it deprives such groups of self-actualizing roles in the administrative process. The problem now becomes one of finding an Aristotelian golden mean, a middle path which will guide us around the pitfalls which centralization and decentralization both present, while advancing us toward the benefits which both have to offer.

Fortunately, such a path exists and so do some guideposts which point toward it. Paul Appleby, looking back on his experiences as a New Deal bureaucrat, once noted that there can be no sound decentralization until there has first been centralization. "One cannot dispense what one does not actually have." Decentralization must stem "from a core of basic responsibility." More recently, McGeorge Bundy has amplified and buttressed this point. "I hold there is no necessary contradiction between the concept of effective public authority and that of maximum feasible participation," said Bundy in delivering the Godkin lectures at Harvard in 1968. "If you want participation, you must first have something to participate in, and the way to give a share of power to people in these cases is first to give real power to an agency of government. I think the accountable executive is much more likely to afford real participation to the poor—and to other constituencies—when he has some power to share than when he does not."

What these writers have prescribed, empirical evidence seems to confirm. Efforts at meaningful decentralization have usually sprung from higher rather than lower units of government. The move to involve the poor in decision-making for example has more often than not had its impetus from Washington or the state capital than from City Hall. To take another example, consolidation of small governments into metropolitan ones in Nashville, Tennessee and Toronto, Canada has, acording to James Medeiros, assistant professor of political science at Northeastern University, actually *increased* citizen participation in local government. In business, it is large corporations rather than small proprietorships which have taken the most steps toward allowing their employees to participate in profits, ownership, and decision-making. A *certain amount of centralization is actually necessary to insure that the advantages of decentralization will be realized.*

The administrative revolution seeks to achieve this indispensable balance. Its basic philosophy regarding the issue is sometimes expressed in these words: centralization of objectives and decentralization of decision-making. The goals of an organization, be it a business, a government agency, or an entire society, should emanate, once all the inputs from the field have been made, from the center. But the decisions necessary to implement these goals are left to the fullest extent possible to those in the field. Management is by results and not by directive control. The individual is afforded the maximum opportunity to "do his own thing" provided he ends up contributing to the organization's aims and purposes.

The organization's aims and purposes, it should be remembered, cannot be handed down from on high. As we have already seen, the organization must allow its members to contribute to such aims and purposes. Two basic reasons dictate this: with the parts of any organization becoming increasingly specialized, the organization must increasingly rely on inputs from its constituent units if it is to set its goals realistically. And, with workers becoming increasingly professionalized, the organization must increasingly try to elicit their consent and a certain degree of enthusiasm in order to achieve those goals which it does set.

PPBS and planning are fully consistent with this new centralization-decentralization formula. Plannings, as we saw earlier, cannot successfully take place without participation. It cannot also be successfully implemented without decentralized control. It focuses on results not methods, on ends not means. The situation regarding PPBS is similar. The new budgeting method, while it centralizes objectives, makes for less centralized control. The decisional flow, as Allen Schick points out, is "downward-disaggregative" rather than "upward-aggregative." What he means is that once the objectives have been set, they are parcelled out to the field or subunits for implementation. Lump sum budgeting becomes facilitated under PPBS for now it becomes unnecessary and even counterproductive to scrutinize separate items of expenditure from above. It's the results that count. At the same time, the subunits may proceed knowing that they are not working at cross-purposes with other subunits or with the overall organization. And, since the organization does set the objectives and does hold its constituent units accountable for them, it can more easily be held accountable by the press, the public, and other institutions of society.

What about the impact of computers and the other modern devices which speed communication? In a sense they make centralization easier but also, in a sense, they make it less necessary. Research at Carnegie Institute of Technology indicates that modern communications networks only lead toward centralization of routine tasks. M.I.T. management Professor Donald C. Carroll claims that a centralized data base and decision programs may make centralization less useful than previously, because a subunit can now have access on its own to information needed when it makes a decision that will have an organization-wide impact. Consequently, decisions which once had to be passed up to a higher level can now be made further down.

Similarly, the trend toward large-scale organization may actually spur decentralization or at least the values which decentralization is designed to foster. In 1959, Harlan Cleveland replied to those who had expressed fears of the humanity-crushing effects of emerging organizational dinosaurs. Precisely because big organizations make most of the vital decisions affecting our destiny, more people are participating in those decisions than ever before, he argued. "The number of decisions that *are* important to our individual lives is multiplying so rapidly that it takes a growing proportion of the nation's available leadership to get them made at all." Concluded Cleveland, "the result of bigness is actually a diffusion of the decision-making and decision-influencing process far beyond the wildest dreams of those . . . who wanted to keep power diffused by keeping the units of society small."

The same theme has been more recently voiced and documented by Max Ways. Making foreign policy, points out Ways,

> was a relatively simple matter in the days when the Monroe Doctrine was quietly born. Since the whole Washington staff of the Department of State was then made of ten clerks and two messengers, internal clearance presented no difficulty. Today a policy mile-stone of like import would have to be cleared at hundreds of points—not all of them official. Dozens of very-high-level hours would have to be spent

defending the new policy to Joe Alsop. Meanwhile the White House would worry over what would be the reaction of William Fulbright, Johnny Carson, the Friends of Uruguay, the League of Women Voters of Tampa, the United Nations Delegate from Tanzania, and the Foreign Policy Study Group of Winnetka High.

A final and now familiar factor of modern society which is fostering decentralization is the familiar one of change. Centralization cannot cope with conditions of rapid change. It takes too long to pass decisions up to the top and it becomes too difficult for the top to make them once they are received. Flexibility and speed are becoming increasingly vital in modern administration and so is the decentralized decision-making which nurtures such qualities. "Change will be too fast-moving, too pervasive, too varied," said the General Electric study on the future business environment, "for it to be dealt with on a centralized, monolithic basis." We may therefore look forward to seeing the positive values with which decentralization has long been associated grow and thrive as the administrative revolution progresses.

THE NEW DECENTRALIZATION AT WORK

The drive for decentralization is accelerating throughout the industrialized world. True, like most emerging ideas it has so far produced more talk than action but it has nonetheless already yielded very tangible results. Even France, where centralization has long been an enshrined principle, is bowing to the winds of change. It used to be said that the French Minister of Education could look at his clock and know from telling the time just what verb every fifth grade child in the country was learning to conjugate at that moment. Now, slowly but surely such heavy-handed rule from Paris is becoming less and less acceptable, even to Paris itself. Interestingly enough, it was the actual centralization of power by de Gaulle which permitted the government to undertake significant steps in decentralizing the governmental process.

One of the leaders in the decentralization drive in France is the government-owned electric power company, C. G. E. Its administrative director, Ambroise Roux, told the French Parliament's hearings on participation that the firm had divided itself into 50 independent affiliates. Every affiliate is headed by a manager who has wide administrative, financial, technical, and commercial discretion. "At headquarters," boasted Roux, "we have neither technical direction, commerical direction or purchasing service." The essential role of the mother company is to choose the men and judge them on their results. "The advantage of our system is that headquarters can devote itself to planning for the future and only has to exercise an after-the-fact control."

In Italy, the tight grip which Rome has exercised over the country's administrative apparatus is also being relaxed. Italy has divided itself into 20 regions and, in 1970, began transferring to these regions administrative discretion in such areas as urban planning, retail trade regulation, etc. "A businessman in Tuscany who wants a state-guaranteed low-interest loan to build a hotel will henceforth apply to the new regional administration in Florence instead of to Rome," commented *The New York Times* in reporting on the change.

The USSR is also feeling the effects of the new trend. In the late 1960s, the Soviets launched an experiment with one of their more technological ministries, the Ministry of Instrument Making Automatic Devices and Control Systems. The experiment called for each of the Ministry's departments to become more independent and to work out jointly with the industries under its control detailed production planning. In 1969, those automation industries that worked under the new arrangement increased production by 19 percent. Just how sweeping a departure such decentralization is for the Russians can be seen by looking at some of their other industries. The Ministry of Meat and Dairy Industries sent its subordinate enterprises and organizations more than 40,000 memoranda during the same year.

In Hungary a new government plan, according to the *New York Times*, "has been reduced to a general guideline that is no longer binding on enterprises. Managers who in the past had to telephone the Ministry in Budapest ten times a day on minor questions now have substantial freedom of decision. Within limits they are free, for instance, to make their own contracts with customers and suppliers of raw material in foreign countries."

The move to administrative decentralization in European countries has not, however, been accompanied by an equal drive towards political decentralization. Indeed, when it comes to political autonomy, the move has often been in the reverse direction. In 1965, Sweden amalgamated its 119 local and regional police forces into one national organization. France the following year did the same with its two principal police forces, the Paris police and the *Sûreté National*. In Germany, the federal government is exercising more and more guidance over the country's educational system which has hitherto been left almost exclusively in the hands of the German states. And the British government is regrouping the country's local governmental units into larger regional ones.

These developments do not negate nor conflict with administrative decentralization but actually enhance it. If police forces feud with each other, as has been the case in France, then overall direction must be coordinated. Otherwise, there will be no valid system of accountability and no way of insuring that the organization can be held responsible by the country. The values which decentralization are designed to attain are thereby jeopardized and frequently frustrated. In private as well as public administration, political or policy-making centralization and administrative decentralization not only complement but aid and abet one another.

In this hemisphere, Canada has shown more understanding of this principle than has the United States. The 1963 report of the Royal Commission on Government Reorganization, known as the Glassco Commission Report, took as its central theme the delegation of more authority to Canada's departments and agencies. The Commission felt they should have more discretion, for example, in both financial and personnel fields. *At the same time,* the Commission called for strengthening and expanding the staff and the services of Canada's Treasury Board Secretariat so that it could better perform its task of advising, evaluating, and coordinating the functions and performance of the national government's departments and agencies.

Toronto's adventuresome experiment in metropolitan government provides a more concrete example of how the new decentralization works. Local school boards have continued to exist and even thrive under the new metropolitan framework. They formulate their own budgets but pass them on to the Metropolitan School Board for approval. Since the local boards also elect representatives to the Metro Board, they are assured of spokesmen in its deliberation. For its part, the Metro Board strives to take into account the special needs and desires of each district. Allocations on a strictly per capita or per pupil basis have been avoided. If the local board still finds itself overruled and feels it has a good case for its spending plans, it has two additional options. It can appeal to the Ontario Municipal Board or it can, within limits, impose an additional tax on its own district. "It's a matter of starting the process from the ground up rather than imposing it from above," one school official told writer Robert Bendiner. The new amalgamated school system, Bendiner found, has generally given increased satisfaction to pupils, parents, and teachers alike. Community involvement in the schools has actually increased.

In this country, it is the private sector which has taken the commanding lead in the administrative decentralization drive. General Motors helped pioneer this movement after its late president, Alfred P. Sloane, noted that "in practically all of our activities, we seem to suffer from the inertia resulting from our great size."

One of the more recent decentralization techniques which business has instituted is the profit center concept. Under this arrangement, a subunit handles most of the functions involved in a given product or group of products. Its manager functions much like the president of a small company but is held responsible for the profit of his center.

While administrative decentralization in the public sector has failed to keep pace, it nevertheless has managed to achieve some gains in recent years. Cities like New York and Boston have set up neighborhood city halls to assist local residents in obtaining administrative services. The California Compensation Insurance Fund is an outstanding example of what some of the more progressive states are doing. The federal bureaucracy is allowing more and more decision-making to be made in the field, and the detailed supervision so long exercised by Washington is starting to ease up. Many field units now enjoy, for example, lump sum budgeting or what amounts to its equivalent, and some can negotiate contracts with private parties.

What has complicated and confused the problem in America is our failure to differentiate properly political from administrative centralization. The United States is far and away the most politically decentralized nation in the Western World. There are more than 80,000 governmental subunits in this country and most of them wield a degree of political independence that startles an observer from Europe or Japan.

Even within the subunits, fragmentation of power exists and often seems to run rampant. Governors frequently find themselves powerless to hold their administrative agencies responsible and mayors sometimes have to contend with situations that are almost as bad. It has long been customary for New York City's administrative agencies to act like separate principalities, escaping complete chaos only by making what amounts to treaties with each other. The independence of many parts of the federal bureaucracy has long baffled and undermined even the strongest president. During the 1930s, both the Army Engineers and the Bureau of Reclamation wanted to build the King's River Dam in California. President Roosevelt gave specific orders that the Bureau of Reclamation should do the job. But the Army Engineers built the King's River Dam.

It is for this reason that we see two seemingly contradictory but actually complementary forces at work in American administration at the present time. Mayor John Lindsay, while seeking to strengthen his neighborhood centers and delegate more decision-making power to them, has, at the same time, sought through agency consolidation and stronger budgetary procedures to increase his grip on the city's bureaucracy. Without a strong mayoral control over the bureaucracy, New York's neighborhood city hall program cannot succeed. President Nixon has taken a similar approach. While delegating more decision-making discretion to the federal government's field offices, he has sought to tighten overall coordination and control over the federal bureaucracy by replacing the Bureau of the Budget with a strengthened and expanded Office of Management and Budget. These two steps go hand in hand.

In general we find political power passing upward in the United States at the present time, while administrative discretion is seeping downward. States are manifesting more direction over, and support for, welfare, school, and other hitherto strictly local functions. At the same time, state governments are giving somewhat more discretion to their own field personnel in handling such functions. The federal government is doing likewise. But the trend is as yet uneven and slow-moving. Political decentralization remains embedded too deeply in the American consciousness to be easily dislodged. The result has been not only to retard administrative decentralization, but in some areas, to transform it into its political counterpart.

The best example, perhaps, of this last cited turn of events is the poverty program. Under the battle cry of maximum feasible participation, elections were held in various poverty areas. In no election did more than 10 percent of those eligible vote. In most elections the turnout came to less than 5 percent and in some, less 1 percent. In those instances where elections did not take place, separate power groups formed to battle for the funds. Their jousting for control has led to over a score of murders in New York City, Chicago, and Boston alone.

The final consequence was as expected. Control by elites and vested interests, so characteristic of small-town America, now began to take shape in metropolitan slums. In all probability, less involvement of, and less responsiveness to, slum residents resulted from this form of decentralization than would have been the case had administrators been appointed from above and held responsible for achieving such participatory goals. All too many of the poverty leaders who emerged from the poverty elections or the poverty wars concentrated their efforts at securing generous salaries and emoluments for themselves and their friends. Of the $8 million dispensed ostensibly to help the poor in Syracuse, New York, for example, $7 million was paid out in salaries and much of the remaining $1 million probably never directly helped those for whom it was intended.

The lessons of the poverty program are not new. Years ago when the Department of Agriculture sought to allow local committees to decide by themselves on how to allocate grants, the rich or politically astute farmers ended up getting all the money. (To some extent, they still do.) A system of accountability to a higher level remains a vital necessity if decentralization is to achieve *its own goals*. Yet, the learning of such lessons has been slow in coming.

The United States has taken to heart Thomas Jefferson's admonition that "in government, as well as in every other business of life, it is by division and subdivision of duties alone that all matters, great and small, can be managed to perfection." However, we have tended to ignore the caution of Alexis de Tocqueville who visited us shortly after Jefferson's death. De Tocqueville wisely noted that "a centralized administration is fit only to enervate the nation in which it exists." But he also pointed out that without a powerful central government, "no nation can live and prosper."

6

THE ERA OF THE CLIENT

For over half a century, the Children's Bureau was a thorn in the side of the federal bureaucracy. It was not that federal bureaucrats didn't believe in helping children. They did. It was not that federal bureaucrats disliked the personnel of the Children's Bureau or disapproved of what they were trying to do. They did not. It was simply that the Bureau wasn't organized correctly and, because of this, it tended to make life difficult for many others on the bureaucratic scene.

Established in 1912, the Children's Bureau marked the federal government's entry into the cause of direct welfarism. Such an entry had been a long time in coming. Social Darwinism and its survival-of-the-fittest philosophy had dominated the political atmosphere in this country since the Civil War, if not before. The notion that the federal government should actually extend direct aid and succor to an individual and thereby deprive him of his independence had, for many Americans, long constituted a horror too gruesome to contemplate. But by 1912 many of the more compassionate were ready to concede that perhaps children could be assisted without robbing them of their moral character and without striking a crippling blow at one of the country's most cherished ideals. Congress, responding to this softening trend and goaded further by growing embarrassment over child labor abuses, enacted the necessary legislation and the federal government's first welfare agency made its debut.

At the outset, there was no dearth of work for the Bureau to do. In addition to child labor problems there was, for example, an extremely high child mortality rate. In those years, one out of ten babies died before it reached its first birthday. The Bureau managed to reduce this mortality rate and to make other contributions to the welfare of the young. It became an established fixture in the federal bureaucracy and grew along with it. Its budget increased from $20,000 at its inception to $260 million in 1968. But the administrative problems it presented also grew and late in 1969, President Nixon finally ended its bothersome existence.

What made the Children's Bureau bothersome? Simply this: its client-oriented structure. Traditionally, most administrative agencies are organized differently. The most common basis of organization is purpose. In this manner, police departments are organized to fight crime, fire departments are organized to fight fires, postal departments are organized to deliver mail. Another and less popular but still acceptable basis of administrative organization is by process. An agency organized on the basis of process is organized in terms of the type of work that it does. An example of such an agency is a city law department which provides legal services to various other municipal agencies but only services of a particular kind.

The Children's Bureau was not organized on either the basis of purpose or process but on the basis of the clientele it served. Its orientation was not to fulfill certain set purposes or to discharge certain types of functions but to service a particular group of clients and to service them in all kinds of ways. It proudly boasted that it did not simply educate, or secure housing for, or arrange medical treatment for, children; instead, it cared for the *whole child*.

When the Children's Bureau was the federal government's only welfare agency, when it stood as a lonely outpost in the bureaucracy disdainful or fearful of providing direct aid to human beings, its administrative structure caused few problems. But as soon as the government began to undertake other welfare activities, trouble arose. It was difficult to carry out comprehensive welfare, educational, or health programs, when the Children's Bureau remained a zealous custodian of an important segment of the people these newer programs were designed to aid. The Bureau just didn't fit on HEW's swollen organizational chart. Furthermore, state and local officials frequently complained that the existence of the Bureau unnecessarily made life difficult for them. It required them to make separate applications to obtain certain funds.

The Bureau fought hard to stay in operation—it had acquired its partisans in both Congress and the public—and managed to stay its execution for years. But in October 1969, the axe finally fell. President Nixon dismembered the historic if not venerable agency and parcelled out most of its programs to other HEW units.

In taking this action, Nixon was thought to be striking a blow for good or at least better administration. And, given the operational flow and the organizational setup of HEW, he perhaps was doing just that. But the organizational principle which the Children's Bureau embodied, and which finally caused its downfall, is presently enjoying something of a renaissance. Victory for its opponents, ironically, has almost come too late. Though the Bureau is now dead, the clientele-oriented structure which made it so troublesome for so long is now on the rise and seems destined to play an increasingly greater role in the modern administrative process.

Administrators today are becoming more cognizant of the fact that, in the words of Terry Sanford, "government agencies are mono-professional but people are multi-problemal." Sanford, a former governor of North Carolina, bewails the fact that "the welfare office sees poverty as a problem of welfare, the office of education as a problem of education, health officials as a matter of public health. Each has its programs, its guidelines and criteria—and never the slew shall meet." In his book *Storm over the States*, Sanford notes that the North Carolina Fund once came across a problem-laden family which, over a two-year period, had been worked on by 46 separate government and private agencies.

In the few short years that have passed since Sanford made his observation, the trend in administration has undergone a sharp change. The clientele-oriented organization has come increasingly to the fore. We have already seen this in two of the Theory Y organizations which we examined in Chapter 2. It will be recalled that one of the basic structural changes which the experimental field office of the California State Compensation Insurance Fund inaugurated was to put its operations on a clientele basis. Formerly, the field office was divided up into functional divisions dealing with sales, safety, claims/rehabilitation, and auditing. After reorganization, these functional divisions were replaced by work teams which provide all four services to groups of clients. Arthur D. Little is similarly arranged. Its basic unit is also the work team formed specifically to service a particular client or group of clients. "The client's thinking and needs are the major factors determining the power and limitations of our administrative organization," says the company in the statement it issues to prospective employees.

Further examples of this swing to a client-oriented organizational structure are cropping up in increasing numbers. For all its faults, the federal government's poverty program did recognize the multidimensional aspect of the poverty program and, at least to some extent, sought to treat it by providing a variety of services to a particular group of clients. HEW's division of the elderly is another example of this trend. In a sense, the Department of Housing and Urban Development (HUD) also bears witness to this new emphasis on clientele orientation. HUD is essentially a clientele-directed agency and was established principally to give the cities a voice in the Cabinet. It was designed to fight for the servicing of their wide-ranging needs.

The same trend is also underway at lower levels of government. In 1969, the Massachusetts legislature voted to reorganize the state's executive branch, consolidating 173 direct reporting units and 132 near-independent subunits into 11 cabinet offices and a Department of Staff Services. One of the basic arguments used to secure adoption of this change was the need to make the state's bureaucracy more clientele-focused. It was pointed out that while there were 2,000 trained employees to help problem families, they often worked independently of each other. Consequently, the family's entire problem structure never received the comprehensive examination and treatment which it required and deserved. By grouping most of these services into a new consolidated department, it would be possible to service the whole family.

At the municipal level, the trend to clientele orientation has frequently taken the form of decentralization. The neighborhood city halls and other field services which cities are increasingly trying to provide are examples of this. Through concentration of services according to neighborhood, the city more directly acknowledges and responds to the client and his diverse needs. At least three cities have also established commissions on the aging to coordinate and provide a spectrum of separate services for their senior citizens.

Within various purpose-oriented or process-oriented institutions we find client-oriented subunits starting to emerge. Boston's famed Children's Medical Center, for example, has formed a unit which delivers a variety of services to retarded children. Formerly, such youngsters received orthopedic care in one section of the hospital, neurological care in another, psychiatric treatment in yet another, and so forth. Now they need be taken to only one organization unit for all their medical needs.

The new emphasis on clients, however, has not confined itself to structural change alone. It is injecting vast sections of public administration with a new spirit. It is stimulating organizations to undertake new activities and to initiate new approaches to their existing programs.

The Planned Program Budgeting System (PPBS) itself exemplifies this shift. Through its concentration on program effectiveness and results, it brings the client much more to the forefront in an agency's operations than was previously the case. Traditional line-item budgeting, we should recall, tends to concentrate on the accumulation of resources and the carrying on of routine operations. It all too often is concerned with doing things cheaply rather than effectively, and on doing them whether or not they should be done at all. It is one thing for a sanitation agency to receive an allocation to buy so many sanitation trucks and hire so many sanitation men. It is another thing for a sanitation agency to be given a lump sum with the explicit understanding that the garbage shall be picked up and the streets maintained at a certain level of cleanliness. Under PPBS, the services that the agency is supposed to deliver for its clients is now put on the books alongside the dollar amounts involved. And how it is actually meeting a direct client need is kept constantly in mind.

Administrators themselves are becoming increasingly aware that they have a new role to play. "One way in which the federal executive of the future will be different," said the then chairman of the United States Civil Service Commission John Macey in 1968, is that "he will identify more with his constituency—the people to be served by his programs." And Macey quoted with warm approval another writer's statement that "the federal career executive should be just as much a representative of the people as a legislator." Many embattled bureaucrats are not seeking to play this role, but are finding it thrust upon them. Others are accepting it with willingness and even fervor. We see examples of it everywhere. In the planning profession, a new movement called "Advocacy Planning" has leaped into prominence. It calls on planners to become spokesmen in the planning process for groups which are often thought to lack adequate advocates for their interest and views. Welfare workers, teachers, and others, including top-level administrators, are also becoming spokesmen and fighters for those they serve.

As part of this changing trend, administrators are not only doing more listening to their clients but are setting up administrative devices to encourage the clients to talk. Polls are one of the tools sometimes employed to find out what the clients actually want. Another device is the advisory committee. HEW now has over 200 such committees in operation. The federal government itself in October 1969 set up in Philadelphia the first of what is to be a network of "listening posts" throughout the country to elicit, receive, and process suggestions and complaints from citizens. All such suggestions and complaints are to receive replies within 14 days. City governments such as New York and Boston have expanded their complaint-processing activities into 24-hour operations with top municipal officials taking turns serving as "night mayor" at City Hall.

This new impetus to client consultation frequently takes interesting forms and directions. The New York State Liquor Authority (SLA) has always given heed—some would say too much heed—to the liquor concerns which it regulates. But in November 1969, the liquor agency held its first meeting with a citizens committee of drinkers and non-drinkers which it had organized to provide it with the views of its broader constituency, the public. Called the Advisory Committee on the Public Interest, the citizens group spent three hours with SLA officials discussing such matters as rules for tavern conduct, penalties for sales to minors, duty-free discount sales of imported liquor, and other matters.

"We want the benefits of the ideas and suggestions of this large body of citizens," declared SLA chairman Donald S. Hostetter. "That is the essence for this broadly representative new committee." He said he and other SLA commissioners expected to meet with the committee at least twice a year from now on.

The same trends toward increased clientele consideration are also starting to surface in other western nations. When Dr. Horst Schmidt took office as Minister of Health, Labor and Social Welfare in the West German state of Hesse in the fall of 1969, he made such consideration his first order of business. The first memo he sent to his colleagues and staff instructed them to adopt a "basically friendly" approach to all and sundry who came before them. Those who write should receive prompt replies, said Schmidt, and if their requests have to be refused, then the dismissal should not be made in a peremptory manner. Instead, the administrator should explain as fully as possible in writing the grounds of his refusal. Even people who are being difficult, Schmidt emphasized, should be handled with patience, good humor, and, as far as possible, friendliness. The memo was believed to be the first of its kind ever to issue forth from the labyrinthine recesses of German bureaucracy.

The French bureaucracy which, like the German, has also never been celebrated for dealing with its clients in a warm friendly manner, is likewise showing the signs of the times. The new Pompidou government has strongly emphasized what it calls *concertation* or the building of harmony. To that end, it has and is urging its ministers to establish dialogue between officials and various groups of people.

Prime Minister Jacques Chaban-Delmas has taken the lead by appointing a special state secretary in his own office and charged him with the task of listening to, and reporting on the citizenry's concerns. Jacques Baumel, the 51-year-old Gaullist politician entrusted with the post, receives and responds to 50 to 150 complaints and suggestions by mail every day. In addition, he studies newspapers and other organs of information, goes on radio programs to answer listeners' questions directly, and makes frequent tours of the countryside talking not only with mayors and bureaucrats but also with workers, pensioners, housewives, and students.

"The French felt that they were not enough listened to, that they were isolated," says Baumel. He calls himself the ear of the government and adds "my ears have been getting bigger all the time."

But listening to clients, welcome though it is, is not enough for these revolutionary times. Administrative agencies are learning to respond as well. And increasingly this response is taking the form of giving their clients "a piece of the action." The current popularity of this phrase in itself attests to the growing vigor of the administrative revolution or at least to the vigor of the pressures which are spurring it on. Clients increasingly want more than just a chance to be heard. They are demanding a say in the running of agencies that serve them. And increasingly, they are getting it.

Urban renewal provides one illustration of the step-by-step progression through which the clientele role in governmental operations is expanding. When the program started out after World War II, little if any attempt was made to obtain, much less heed, the wishes of the residents of urban renewal areas. By the early 1960s, however, the situation had markedly changed. Urban renewal staffs were now setting up and consulting with committees from their project areas. In 1968, HUD took steps to formalize and strengthen the role of these committees. It agreed that henceforth such agencies could wield substantive powers and could receive funds for staff of their own. The following summer, the first committee set up under the new plan took office in Boston's

South End. It was given the power to veto any demolition or any contractor in its project area. It was also provided with sufficient funds to maintain an office and employ an executive secretary and a secretary.

Other agencies, acting perhaps on the "if-you-can't-lick-'em, join-'em" principle, have moved to make their clients part of their work force. This has given rise to the paraprofessional movement which is currently mushrooming throughout the country. By the end of the 1960s, some 300,000 former clients were working part- or full-time in public schools, hospitals, and health services and their number was steadily growing. They were winning increasing respect and even acclaim for their efforts.

Dr. Francine Soley of Columbia University's School of Social Work studied the use of over 10,000 such paraprofessionals on 185 projects which the National Institute of Mental Health sponsored from 1960 to 1967. She found that the nonprofessionals put in as much as eight times the man hours of the professionals and performed functions which their sponsoring agencies had previously not provided. They showed "more flexibility, spontaneity, more genuine human commitment than their professional colleagues," she found, although she hastened to point out that the professionals were certainly not lacking such qualities themselves. Furthermore they often scored remarkable success in getting other social institutions to listen and respond to them and to their clients. A judge would frequently respect a paraprofessional's advice more than he would a social worker's when it came, say, to reducing a jail sentence for a client.

The use of paraprofessionals offers a variety of benefits to a variety of parties. It enables the agency to form a stronger link with its clients through the utilization of a person whose background is similar. The clients themselves often find it easier to deal with agency clientel representatives than with the agency's professional personnel. And the paraprofessional is helped by receiving income, occupational upgrading, and sometimes even rehabilitation. This last-cited benefit is particularly important in helping criminal offenders. "It has been learned in correction," writes Donald Grant, "that the best way to rehabilitate offender A is to have him try to rehabilitate offender B."

The latest and perhaps most exciting phase of this client-participation movement involves the clients becoming administrators themselves. In many cities, tenants of housing projects have won appointment to the housing authority boards and some cities are getting ready to turn over the actual operations of housing projects to those who live in them. In

St. Louis, a tenant group is already operating, and operating successfully, an 11-story housing project named after Martin Luther King. Detroit hopes to go further and actually to sell its public housing units to those who inhabit them. In Boston boards of community residents now run newly organized health centers in the city's South End-Roxbury section. These boards screen all personnel and set policy. In New York City, a board of 25 slum mothers is planning the program and hiring the employees for ten neighborhood centers designed to furnish family planning advice and limited prenatal care to impoverished residents of the Bronx. The operating staff itself will consist of local women who will be trained as paraprofessionals at a New York medical school.

Even what has been one of the most closely knit and insulated government institutions, the police, are starting to give their clients a say and a role in their operations. Police-community relations boards are springing up in neighborhoods throughout the country. While at first they tended to be somewhat perfunctory and ritualistic, serving more as public relations gestures than as organs of meaningful involvement, their role in police policy-making is steadily expanding. And while the police have been much more hesitant about involving clients on a paraprofessional basis, here too some progress is being made. Some American police forces, particularly small ones, have a long record of using citizens as auxiliaries. Slowly some larger cities are starting to do the same. At least seven cities responded to the race riots of the late 1960s by drawing upon the services of young Negro men to patrol their own communities, and a subsequent study by the Lemburg Center for Violence at Brandeis University found such moves, for the most part, to have been successful. In some cases, this has led to permanent police auxiliary organizations being formed. New Rochelle, New York's *Police Partners* program which recruits, trains, and pay Negro youths for assisting in law enforcement, is credited with doing much to alleviate tensions and forestalling further riots in that troubled city.

The trend toward client involvement is one aspect of the administrative revolution in which the United States leads the way. But other nations have certainly not remained immune from its impact. German police forces, for example, are making increasing use of auxiliaries recruited from the very neighborhoods in which they are to be assigned. Sweden is using students at the high school level to help run its educational system. And Japan is using clients to protect other clients.

In 1961 Japan began setting up boards of local administrative counselors to receive and sort out citizen complaints and forward those deserving attention to the proper authorities. These counselors are unpaid but since retirement in Japan, as we noted earlier, comes at 55 years of age, the nation has a large pool of competent volunteers to draw upon. There are now over 3600 such local counselors and, as a result of their efforts, the Japanese are complaining as never before. According to Walter Gelhorn, the number of cases they received and processed rose from 10,000 to 55,000 in their first four years of existence.

In a pioneering work on administration entitled *The Functions of the Executive*, Chester Barnard emphasized that an organization's survival depended on contributions not just from its employees but also from its clients and constituencies. He felt that clients must be viewed as an integral part of the organization. Barnard's insight was a rather novel one for administrative theory when his book was first published in 1938. But the novelty has long since worn off. The clientele role in administration has already reached dimensions far surpassing Barnard's conception and clientele participation promises to become an increasingly vital factor in organizational life as the administrative revolution pushes on.

CLIENTS AS CONSUMERS

"President Nixon has taken the American consumer by the hand and said, in effect, 'we will take care of you.'" So wrote the *Christian Science Monitor* on November 1, 1969 as it reported on a presidential message that had recently gone to Congress. The *Monitor's* rhetoric was somewhat overblown but not fundamentally inaccurate. In submitting its consumer bill, the Nixon administration had apparently made up its mind to gird itself to fight one of the good fights of present-day American politics.

President Nixon's entry into the affray can scarcely be viewed, however as a display of intrepid leadership. After decades, even centuries of neglect, the American consumer by the late 1960s had begun to enjoy a sudden blaze of popularity. All at once the woods had become full of gallant knights ready to do battle in his behalf.

This turn of events represents a far cry from the situation which existed just ten years before. The American consumer movement then consisted of a marginal minority of dedicated people toiling, so it seemed, in the wilderness. No official agency existed at any level of government specifically designed to hear the consumer's cry and champion his cause. But the 1960s changed all that. By the end of the decade the long forgotten man in the drama of American politics had now become the star of the show.

Like all political and social causes that acquire near instant popularity, this one is suspect. Many are inclined to write it off as a passing fancy that will soon lose its zest and impetus, allowing things to return to being pretty much as they were. The number of those scurrying to get aboard the consumer bandwagon is now so great that the bandwagon will, they say, soon collapse under its own weight.

This may be true but there are indications that it is not. While the current consumer drive may lose some of its spark, and while the current headlines it is prompting may shrink in size, the fires it has ignited have a substance to them which makes it unlikely that they will ever go completely out. The consumer is now achieving his long overdue recognition from the country's political, economic, and social system, and the steps being taken would seem to insure that a good measure of his newly acquired recognition will become a built-in feature of our way of life.

The forces of consumerism began to gather under the Kennedy administration. The new president had commissioned Harvard Law School Dean James Landis to make a study of the federal regulatory commissions. Landis found that these commissions, instead of regulating the industries under their supervision, had themselves become regulated by the regulatees. This conclusion was scarcely a new or surprising one. But it was the first time that it had ever been officially submitted and published by an American president. Kennedy responded by seeking to strengthen presidential control over these regulators of the public interest and by trying to appoint more committed members to their boards. During the 1960s, some of these long-sleeping giants began to stir. Particularly noteworthy were the Federal Communications Commission (FCC) and the Securities and Exchange Commission (SEC). The FCC began cracking down on ownership concentration in broadcasting and called for a ban on cigarette advertising. The SEC initiated a series of prosecutions designed to curb the use of inside information in the securities industry.

But though at least some regulatory commissions showed much more life in the 1960s than they had for decades, criticism of their sloth and laxity only mounted in intensity. The regulators' stepped-up efforts—and it must be admitted that such efforts were still nowhere near as stepped-up as they might be—brought only fresh charges that they were lying down on the job. More and more people were joining consumer societies, reading consumer magazines, and becoming concerned over the long neglect of the consumer interest. The war-induced inflation, by rubbing salt on the consumer's financial wounds, only fanned the flames of his discontent. Finally, the motor safety efforts of Ralph Nader, and the efforts of General Motors to counteract him, brought the consumer cause into the limelight and gave the nation's consumers a leader and a champion. Reacting to these and other developments, Congress already had passed a truth-in-lending law and was considering no fewer than 120 other consumer-oriented bills when the President's message arrived.

The President asked Congress for a new Office of Consumer Affairs which would have "legislative standing." He also pleaded with the lawmakers to establish a Division of Consumer Protection in the Department of Justice and to reorganize the Federal Trade Commission (FTC) to make it more vigorous and more accountable to presidential policies. Consumers are being encouraged to file protests with the White House—such complaints were already approaching the level of 2,000 a month—and the White House would be given more power to act upon them.

Whatever happens to the President's consumer bill, and at this writing it seems likely that in one form or another such a measure will pass, other and stronger consumer controls are waiting in the wings. Among the bills before Congress in 1970 was one to broaden and liberalize the rule regarding what are called class action suits in the federal courts. Under a class action, any customer who feels he has been cheated or defrauded can bring suit not only in his own name but in the name of everyone who might have a similar complaint. Consequently, a suit for a paltry couple of hundred dollars could, if successful, cost a company a not-so-paltry couple of hundred thousand dollars or more. The bill, which has bipartisan support from liberals in both parties, has evoked enthusiastic support from consumerism's white knight, Ralph Nader. Says Nader, "this is the real stuff; it is a terrific tool."

Some states, such as California, already permit class action suits and this illustrates another aspect of the consumer movement: it has spread out and embraced all levels of the political system. In certain respects, the states have even surpassed the federal government in their zeal to ride this new political tiger. In 1960 no state in the nation had a consumer affairs office in operation; by 1970 some 33 states had established such agencies and other states were planning to follow suit. It should be emphasized that, for the most part, these new bureaus are not functioning as mere window-dressing operations designed only to give the illusion of action. Maryland, a state which has never been known as a spearhead of progress within the federal system, provides an example of just how important the consumer movement has become in state government.

In 1967, the Maryland legislature passed a bill setting up a Consumer Protection Division in the state's Attorney General's office. Two years later the division had recovered and restored to bilked consumers over one million dollars in money, merchandise, and services. The division had established storefront offices in ghetto areas, four of them in Baltimore alone, to receive complaints. It had distributed information brochures, sponsored talks, and was even offering courses in schools.

The division had also filed numerous consumer-protection bills, many of which had been enacted. Among the latter were measures outlawing debt adjusting, referral selling, and suits filed by purveyors for the return of merchandise sent to clients who hadn't ordered it.

Cities, too, are getting into the consumer act. Most notable among them in this respect is New York. On the last day of 1969, Mayor John Lindsay signed a consumer protection measure giving his administration the right to prosecute any business or person who seeks to victimize the public through deceptive practices. The measure set up a 45-man law enforcement division and invested its commissioner with enforcement and rule-making powers. Needless to say, while all this government activity has been going on, private enterprise has not been idle. Although it has been opposing what it considers to be the most extreme of the consumer defense measures, it has also been taking steps to get its own house in order.

In the two-and-one-half-month period from March 1 to mid-May of 1970, eight national business organizations either held, or announced plans to hold, meetings on the subject of public complaints and what to do about them. At one such meeting, the Association of Home Appliance Manufacturers, the Gas Appliance Manufacturers Association, and the American Retail Federation jointly decided to establish what they called the Major Appliance Consumer Action Panel. The panel's purpose is to handle complaints from consumers who have exhausted the routine procedures of contracting dealers, repair services, and warrantors. The business group selected a university home management professor, Dr. Virginia Cutler, to chair the panel and promised that the group would be "entirely free of industry control or influence." According to Dr. Cutler, the panel would probe each complaint and then go to the manufacturer involved with its final decision. And its final decision would be binding.

Other examples of businesses taking the initiative in responding to the new consumer consciousness turn up almost daily. Applicants for TV stations are now promising to give the public more opportunities to participate in the programming. The New York State Food Merchants Association, confronted with a New York City regulation requiring grocery items to be unit priced, has developed a pocket-sized computer to help housewives figure out these unit prices (unit prices simply mean the cost per unit of merchandize). In the Midwest where no such unit-price regulations yet exist, a supermarket chain, the 22-store Benner Tea Company, has decided to set up a full-scale unit-pricing system on its own. The company's president says the action is taken not for altruistic motives but to make more money. Business has seen the writing on the wall. In the era of the client, such steps can, do, and will pay off.

ADVERTISING AND SALESMANSHIP:
THE CHANGING FACE OF HUCKSTERISM

In the capitalist market place, so the truism once ran, the consumer reigns supreme. But now everyone knows that the truism wasn't true. Consequently, another has taken its place. Current thinking depicts the consumer as a hapless, helpless prey for the dark forces of corporate greed. Hidden persuaders are now thought to lurk under every bush and boulder ready to pounce on him as he blindly tries to thread his way through the jungle of modern marketing.

This new image of the consumer, sophisticaed as it may seem, is no more realistic than the one it replaced. If the consumer is not the supreme sovereign he was once considered, he is also not the supine subject he is now so often portrayed. Furthermore, he is likely to become still less of a powerless pawn in the future. As we have already seen, the consumer is flexing his muscles and raising his voice as never before. As we will now see, he is being aided and abetted by various forces in modern society which are changing the function, scope, and even purposes of marketing.

We can examine these new developments best, perhaps, by centering on two specific areas: salesmanship in general and advertising in particular. Dealing with them separately will entail some overlap but will also provide more detail. Given the vast changes taking place in marketing, such a detailed look is fully warranted.

One of the first trends to note is the decline of direct sales personnel as a percentage of the labor force. This has been going on for some time and promises to continue. It has been most noticeable in the retail industry as big stores have replaced small ones, as chain operations have replaced individual proprietorships, and as supermarket operations have replaced direct sales methods. The trend has been noticeable in industry as well. A study of 518 manufacturing firms in Bavaria, Germany, showed that from 1960 to 1969 the proportion of marketing employees decreased 2.5 percent. Marketing analyst E. B. Weiss, writing in *Advertising Age* in June 1970, says "in twenty years I expect the nation's sales force to be halved. And that may turn out to be a conservative projection."

What forms the basis for Weiss's sweeping prognosis? He lists about 25 reasons including rising cost, growing reluctance of men to accept such employment because of its status, low work satisfaction, family pressures, and new techniques of purchasing. Among the latter, he cites the growing resort to committees and the growing use of computers in making purchasing decisions.*

The shrinking number of employees per customer sales in itself reduces the possibilities for manipulation. There is simply less time and manpower available to carry out such stratagems. But another factor which springs from the same source as the reduced number of sales personnel, namely the trend toward larger enterprises and chain operations, adds impetus to this decline. Large firms simply find it harder to

---

* One of Weiss's 25 reasons is especially interesting in view of what we noted earlier concerning centralization. He says "the mounting organizational complexities of giant corporations" makes it extremely difficult for the salesmen to identify the point of decision . . . "The decentralization of buying decisions further complicates the situation."

control their sales force and to induce them to engage in unscrupulous behavior. The large firm must adopt more standardized and formal procedures and must communicate them to large groups of employees, usually in writing. In these circumstances, outright chicanery becomes increasingly difficult. Large firms are also much more visible and much more vulnerable to pressures from governmental agencies and consumer organizations. It is obviously easier to keep tabs on, and bring pressure against, ten large firms than it is several hundred small ones. Finally, the managers of large firms, while certainly profit-minded, are, at the same time, more conscious of the long-range and broader consequences of their acts.

None of this is meant to imply that size in itself gives a business firm a clean bill of health in terms of its behavior toward consumers. But it does mean that the larger firm is less apt to engage in deplorable consumer practices than is its smaller counterpart. In the words of Philip MacDonald, Associate Professor of Marketing Management at Northeastern University, "The shift toward large-scale commercial operations unquestionably reduces, though it does not eliminate, the worst forms of consumer exploitation." Second, because a large organization tends to establish prescribed rules and regulations, often putting them in written form. It is hard to imagine stores like Macy's or Woolworth's instructing their salesmen on how to pull a fast one on their customers. Transmitting such information and instruction to such a large group would almost certainly make it mandatory for it to be put in written form or at least to be presented at a large gathering. The news would soon leak out and a disastrous backlash would doubtlessly ensue. Most, though certainly not all, consumer frauds are perpetrated by small enterprises, particularly marginal ones such as those often found in ghetto areas.

Many people today bemoan the depersonalization which has often crept into large-scale operations and mourn for the friendly service which the local merchant used to provide. However, one should remember that all too often while the corner butcher was inquiring sympathetically after the customer's health, his thumb was quietly pressing on the scale which was weighing the customer's meat.

Large-scale operations not only have less opportunity to cheat but also less motivation to do so. Harry Levinson points out that when a firm encourages its employees to cheat its customers, it is also encouraging them to cheat the firm itself. One cannot foster a certain pattern of behavior and expect that it will limit itself to any one area of activity. Once a salesman becomes accepting of, and adroit at, the utilization of dishonest techniques, he has few compunctions about applying them to all his business relationships.

But, as Weiss has indicated, even where businesses specially instruct their salesmen to manipulate customers they are finding it harder to recruit salesmen who are willing to do so. Not only cheating but all forms of high pressure hucksterism are going out of style. Customer resistance is too great and the work itself is considered too degrading to tempt and retain the modern salesman—who is a far cry from his predecessor.

Around the turn of the century, notes Philip McDonald, 80 or 90 percent of all salesmen in this country were on straight commission. Today, he estimates, no more than 20 percent are even predominately on commission, and the proportion is shrinking all the time. As a matter of fact, companies are increasingly dropping the word "salesman" from their vocabulary and are using such terms as customer representative or sales engineer to take its place.

The use of these new terms, it should be pointed out, is not merely an attempt to slap a new label on an old bottle. The bottle itself has changed, and so has its contents. Selling in the technological society frequently involves a continuing relationship. The day has passed, says Professor McDonald, when a firm could create a product and then tell its salesmen to go out and peddle it. Instead, it sends out its men to ask about the customers' needs and then attempts to see if it can come up with something to meet those needs. As one IBM vice president has said, "we don't sell a product; we sell solutions to problems." Working out such solutions involves many months or even years. Highhanded selling methods simply won't work in such a situation.

As a result of such changes, the abilities which companies look for, and seek to develop in their sales personnel, are also changing. The modern salesman is more and more of a specialist and even a technician. The products he sells, and the people he sells them to, are no longer amenable to the glad-handing, back-slapping methods of old. He must understand complicated products and complicated problems and try to match one with the other.

Salesmen themselves are becoming increasingly conscious of this change. A survey of practitioners conducted by Opinion Research Corporation found that "salesmen complain that their training focuses far too much on the simple mechanics of the selling situation; how to dress, how to greet the prospect, how to make the clothes, etc.; and pays insufficient attention to the more sophisticated problems which they must be able to handle today." The salesmen cited the special marketing problems of their customers as the area where they would most like further education. Basic selling techniques finished near the bottom of the list of what they felt were their educational needs.

The changing character of sales conventions offers another way of measuring this metamorphosis. The liquor still flows at such gatherings but much less copiously than it did in times past. Those attending such conventions today are devoting increasing amounts of time and attention to finding out about new ideas and new techniques. Some sales conventions now resemble a series of graduate school seminars.

Finally, the literature designed for salesmen bears witness to this changing trend. The lead article in the June 1970 issue of *Salesman's Opportunity,* a magazine of short punchy pieces long-geared to the interests and needs of hard-sell salesmen, is a case in point. Entitled "How to Fight Consumer Resistance," the article begins by acknowledging the growing consumer movement and the increasing government regulation which it is generating. "We are selling in an era of greater consumer awareness, sophistication and caution," says the author, Russell J. Formwalt. "No longer is the customer satisfied with an attractive box. Sure, he wants a colorful package, but he wants it to contain a full measure of good quality oatmeal or candy."

Formwalt's advice is tailored to meet these new standards. "Eliminate claims that are hard to substantiate. Delete promises which you aren't sure you can keep. Place more emphasis on the needs and interests of your prospects." And he makes it quite clear that, in his view, such standards of operation are the best and perhaps the only way of now achieving success. "The most potent weapon in your selling arsenal is simple honesty," he emphasizes as he instructs the modern day salesman on how to make it in the modern world.

If the old-time salesman is going the way of the vaudevillian whom he so often resembled, another form of hucksterism appears to have taken his place. Expenditures on advertising have risen rapidly in recent years and many regard the members of the industry as the master manipulators of all time. The alarm was first sounded, or at least loudly sounded, by Vance Packard in his book *The Hidden Persuaders.* The theme has since been taken up by others, among them John Kenneth Galbraith.

In his best selling book, *The New Industrial State*, Galbraith showed that he had swallowed Packard's thesis and swallowed it whole. Advertising and its related techniques have become for Galbraith the major molds in which the supposedly omnipotent business organization of today shapes the consumer's taste to its own will and whim. Thanks to advertising, he argues, today's consumer doesn't stand a chance. Furthermore, Galbraith appears to feel that this is the natural course of events in our modern age. "In the more technological and more complex society, the sovereignty of the individual gives way to the producing organization," he has since said (in a speech at Northeastern University, in 1970).

The idea has struck a responsive cord in the minds and hearts of many socially-concerned citizens. It is quite understandable why it should. Certainly, the commercials which disrupt our TV shows and the billboards which litter our landscape offer cause for dismay if not despair. Certainly, advertising seems more extensive and more oppressive now than it did years ago. Certainly, the gamut of social horrors ranging from cigarette smoking to tailfins which characterize our society would seem to have been encouraged if not fostered by advertising.

However, as with most social phenomena, the function and impact of advertising is much more complex than appearances indicate. One of the first things to note is that advertising bases itself on market research. And market research bases itself on finding out what the consumer wants and what he will respond to. Over 20,000 people in the United States today are engaged in trying to discover just what the felt needs of the buying public are, and it is upon their discoveries that new products are usually created and advertised. Contrary to the Packard-Galbraithian thesis, products are not just hatched at will by the producing company and palmed off to the public through clever commercials. Whenever this has been attempted, disaster has often ensued.

The classic case that is frequently referred to in this connection is the Edsel, the brainchild of the Ford Motor Company that burst on the scene in the late 1950s in a blaze of souped-up salesmanship and soon disappeared. This, however, was not the first time the giant motor company experienced a marketing setback. A few years prior to the Edsel, Ford had sought to introduce seat belts and other safety features in its cars. Failing to get the American public to buy them, it had to retreat.

In truth, the annals of advertising are filled with costly failures. Around the time the Edsel was living its brief life, champale beer and chemise dresses also made their debuts. Both failed to survive. The chemise is particularly interesting because the women's fashion industry is often thought to be particularly susceptible to manipulation through publicity and advertising campaigns. However, not only does the chemise disaster illustrate the reverse but, more graphically and more recently, so does the case of the mini skirt. This new fashion was created by an obscure young British designer and was frowned upon and opposed by the fashion industry. Yet, it gave Britain its only world-wide conquest since World War II.

In the Fall of 1970, it became evident that the fashion industry was heading for another fiasco. Despite a high-pressure sales campaign, it failed to persuade American women to exchange their short skirts for longer ones. By October, retailers confronted racks upon racks of unsold midi skirts.

Lest it be thought that these are only exceptions, various studies exist which show that they are not. According to Professor Philip Kotler, the commodity drop-out rate is surprisingly high. He cites one study which shows that 80% of all marketed products fail to achieve commercial success. Another survey, he notes, indicates a failure rate of 89%. All the studies concur, he says, in showing "that a significant, probably a substantial, percentage of new products fail." Professor Edgar A. Pessemeir, another expert in marketing, agrees. Pessemier cites a survey which disclosed that "even among powerful and well-managed companies, seven out of eight hours devoted to technical product development by scientists and engineers are spent on products that fail at some stage in the process."

Advertising is not only indicted for supposedly creating synthetic wants for unneeded products but is also held responsible for making us so oriented to, and greedy for, commodities in general. However, here too a *caveat* is in order. Western Europeans hungered for cars and the other durables of the supposedly good life long before they received any appreciable amount of exhortation via advertising to buy them. Today, East Europeans, living in an essentially advertising-free society, are said to be experiencing similar desires. Russia makes no attempt to urge or encourage her citizens to buy cars but the citizens want them and want them avidly just the same. Residents of nearly all communist countries have shown a willingness to make great financial sacrifices to buy expensive cars, refrigerators, etc., despite the fact that no commercials exist to goad them into doing so.

Finally, it should be pointed out that advertising does fulfill some social purpose in providing needed information. It may not perform this function as restrainedly or as reliably as many of us would like, but it does perform this function and consumers might be worse, rather than better off, if the function was not performed at all. In the late 1930s the liberal millionaire Marshall Field established a liberal newspaper in New York City called *PM*. One of *PM*'s laudable features was that it would accept no advertising whatsoever. However, this decision hurt rather than helped the fledgling journal in its quest for readership. Soon it had to publish columns of shopping news to make up for the ads which its readers wanted and seemed to need.

With all these factors in mind, it can be said that advertising has not borne quite as much responsibility for our social ills and misdemeanors as its accusers so often claim. It certainly has contributed to some of our excesses but it does not bear the sole blame for creating them. Nor does it provide the basic mainstay for their support and continuation. Furthermore, if advertising were to be abolished completely, something else would have to be found to take its place.

The question now remains as to its future. Will it play a greater or lesser role in modern society? Will the clientele focus that characterizes the administrative revolution find advertising a more or less troublesome factor in the years to come?

It seems likely that the heyday of advertising is ending and that its impact and influence will decline considerably, possibly even sharply, in the coming era. While advertising will continue to function, several factors point to its curtailment and containment in the coming decades.

The most apparent of these trends is the growth in government expenditures. As we have seen, governmental spending has been rising faster than total spending and there is every indication that it will continue to do so at least during the 1970s. The public sector creates little need for, and makes little use of, advertising. As it consumes a greater portion of the country's resources, it reduces the proportion in which advertising can be utilized. As people spend more of their income, chiefly through taxes, on public goods, they will have proportionately fewer dollars to surrender to the blandishments of billboards and brochures.

Within the private sector itself, however, changes are also underway which should further shrink the proportion of dollars going to advertising. First, there is the growth of the private sector's own service industries. While many private services lend themselves to being advertised, many others do not. Many of the growing number of professionals to whom we are increasingly going for private services are not even allowed to advertise.

Another trend within the private sector which may weaken the influence of advertising is the increasing proportion of funds spent on investment. In an innovating and technological society, growth and the investment to finance it take on added import. This trend tallies with another, namely the increase in skilled, semiprofessional, and professional workers. These groups enjoy greater income, and the greater the income a person receives the greater the proportion of it he is likely to save or invest. This has long been a basic rule of economics. Consequently, the stepped-up demand for investment, combined with the increasing numbers of people who tend to set aside increasing proportions of their income for saving and investment, should reduce the scope of advertising still more.

The changes in the composition of the work force will tend to affect advertising adversely in still another way. With more education, people become more sophisticated. They tend to be less vulnerable to advertising techniques and even less oriented to product consumption. This is doubly true of their children as the news from the campuses these days so vividly illustrates. Commodity fetishism is not like Othello's jealousy; increase of appetite does not grow on what it feeds. After some years of gorging, the zeal for commodity consumption tends to burn itself out. This is why the hunger for consumer goods is less in advertising-saturated United States today than it is in most underdeveloped and communist countries.

Finally, business itself may experience a growing disinclination to make as extensive use of advertising as it has in the past. Advertising gets to be self-defeating after a while with everyone running madly just to remain in the same place. The more commercials and billboards there are, the less impact each of them has. When the FCC announced plans early in 1969 to ban cigarette advertising from television, the shares of cigarette manufacturers on the New York Stock Exchange shot up in price. The sudden rush of buyers was quite logical. During the previous year, the companies had spent $225 million on TV ads principally to compete with each other. The proposed ban thus looked like a godsend for their earnings statements. Today, business in both Europe and the United States is confronting a severe liquidity squeeze, that is, a shortage of cash. Such bonanzas as that given the cigarette companies by the FCC will become increasingly welcome as they struggle to meet the demands for liquidity and growth.

The Packard-Galbraith thesis regarding the omnipotence of advertising makes good demonology but not good sense. It overstates the manipulative machinations of advertising and exaggerates their impact. And Galbraith's contention that such evil forces acquire greater scope and power in the technological society rests more on fantasy than fact. The technological society brings into being a complex of forces that eventually tend to lower rather than raise the voice of hucksterism. The popularity of Galbraith's own thesis attests to this. The fact that advertising is increasingly on the defensive in our increasingly technological society attests to the change in attitudes and procedures which such a society engenders.

"The poor," wrote George Bernard Shaw in his preface to *Major Barbara*, "want very much to wallow in all the costly vulgarities from which the elect among the rich turn away with loathing. It is by surfeit and not by abstinence that they will be cured of their hankering after unwholesome sweets." In our increasingly affluent, service-oriented, educated, and technological society, we will find ourselves increasingly satiated and cured of "hankering after unwholesome sweets." In the process, we are increasingly compelling the private sector to treat us less as obedient subjects and more as willfull sovereigns whose collective voice must be heeded.

THE CITIZEN AS CLIENT OF THE ADMINISTRATIVE STATE

The next revolutions will without doubt be led against administration and not against political power.

It is with this arresting thought that Charles Debbasch, a French professor of administrative law, begins his book *l'administration au pouvoir*. Published in 1969, Debbasch's work sounds a tocsin over the growth of the administrative process. It is administration, not politics, which constitutes the chief threat of modern times, says the author, and he itemizes the many ways in which administration and administrators seem to be assuming control over modern man. His book concludes with an urgent plea for greater curtailment and control over this development lest we are all lost.

One must grant the veracity of Debbasch's thesis that the administrative side of government has grown and grown voluminously. The administrative state has now arrived and shows no signs of withering away. But does its emergence pose a chilling threat to human freedom, dignity and security? Will its growth undermine all the changes which the administrative revolution is bringing to the status and role of the citizen-client?

One of the first things to note in attempting to answer this question is the rather ancient vintage of the fears which prompt it. Debbasch's book starts out, as a matter of fact, with a quotation which reads "it is the power that administers more than the political power which governs that now requires limitations and controls." The man who made this particular statement was Joseph Fievée who lived from 1769 to 1839.

In this century, an English writer authored a book in the late 1920s entitled *The New Despots*. These new despots, according to this writer, were the mushrooming number of civil servants who, he felt, were threatening Britain with a new and fearful tyranny. At around the same time, a leading American business journal published an editorial stressing the urgency of keeping this country's civil service ineffective lest it become dangerous!

We see, then, that such fears are by no means new. We can gain some idea of how justified they are by examining what has happened since these prophets of peril first sounded their fire bells in the night.

For one thing, we note that while the administrative state has grown, control and restraints on the state have grown along with it. Many of the things that we have already examined bear this out. PPBS, clientele-involvement, administrative decentralization, etc., all tend to curb the growth of administrative despotism.

Other, more direct devices, have also come into prominence. The institution of the ombudsman started out in 19th century Scandinavia as a way of insuring that citizens receive fair treatment before government agencies. In recent years, this office of administrative control has taken root in a number of other countries including Canada, Great

Britain, Australia, New Zealand, and a growing number of German cities. It is becoming popular in the United States as well. Hawaii and New York's Nassau County now have full-fledged ombudsmen to investigate citizen complaints. A host of other American governmental bodies are getting ready to join them. In July 1970, for example, four New Jersey communities received grants from their state government to set up ombudsman offices.

Ombudsmen, it should be noted, do more than just respond to complaints. They frequently investigate matters on their own initiative and often suggest basic reforms for improving the delivery of public services. Schonfield praises Scandinavian ombudsmen for "pushing modern administration beyond mere justice toward the recognition of the duty of active kindness."

Other devices and procedures for insuring administrative control have also developed with the growth of administrative activity. Writing at the end of the 1950s, Brian Chapman noted that the French Conseil d'Etat or Administrative Court had "gradually shifted its position in favor of the private citizen." In 1953, the Conseil stopped the government from barring some suspected communist students from entering the National Academy of Administration. And in 1957, the Conseil struck down a government attempt to do the same thing to some students who were thought to favor Algerian independence.

Administrative law itself has grown rapidly in recent decades and its growth has been almost entirely in the direction of broadening the rights of clientele. The right to a hearing, for instance, has been extensively increased. In 1970 the United States Supreme Court granted such a right to any welfare client deprived of benefits. A short time later, a federal district judge in New York conferred such a right on any prisoner subjected to severe disciplinary punishment by custodial authorities. In the latter case, a prisoner being held in solitary confinement for attempting to mail legal papers for a fellow inmate secured a federal court order which ended his isolated incarceration.

It is not only the evolution of administrative law which has brought the citizen increasing protection from governmental power. Developments in criminal law have been equally sweeping and, perhaps, equally important. Since World War II, most Western countries, along with Israel and Japan, have greatly expanded the rights of criminal suspects and defendants and greatly curtailed the powers of policemen and prosecutors. At no time in history has it ever been harder to convict an innocent man of a crime. Furthermore, punishments for those convicted have steadily diminished in severity. Capital as well as corporal punishments are rarely invoked in modernized countries these days. This certainly includes the United States where many state governments still have capital punishment in their statutes but resort to it with steadily decreasing frequency.

It is interesting to note the changes which the agency that has long been the chief arm of governmental despotism, the police, have undergone since the fears of governmental despotism were voiced in the 1920s. In most modern countries the police have increasingly and often eagerly built up the positive side of their functions. Germany's postwar police forces have taken as their motto "the Policemen—Your Friends and Helpers" and have sought to put it into effect with a host of enterprising programs. In Sweden, police patrol cars now carry tools, gasoline, and other things designed to help a motorist in distress. The police in this country have been somewhat slower to respond to this new approach to their function but here too signs of change are starting to emerge. Police-community relations programs, as previously noted, are gradually beginning to add substance to form and in more and more cities, police are serving as trained family dispute counselors, juvenile athletic directors, crime prevention advisors, etc.

Stepping back to get a broader view, we see how society itself has become much more free and much less restrictive with the development of the administrative state. One wonders if this dual development is a mere coincidence. As administration has grown so have the rights of the citizen. This includes the right to indulge in divorce, abortion, pornography, homosexual relations, gambling, and other once-taboo activities. People not yet middle-aged can remember when it was almost impossible in the United States to attack such sacred institutions as churches, the Constitution, and the Daughters of the American Revolution in any public forum or over the broadcast media. Watching TV today, a foreign observer sometimes gets the impression that such dissenting viewpoints are, if anything, more readily accommodated than more conventional ones. Dissenters must now frequently resort to coercion and destruction in order to stir the "establishment" into taking action. The administrative state and the permissive society have flourished in tandem.

This trend, it should be emphasized, is by no means limited to the United States. As a matter of fact, those countries where the administrative state has forged ahead faster than in the United States, such as Sweden and Denmark, have even achieved greater levels of tolerance and permissiveness. And even those states which we have long considered somewhat more authoritarian reflect this trend. In France, for example, Mrs. Judith Miller, a radical philosophy professor at the University of Vincennes had no trouble during the late 1960s promulgating Maoist ideas in her courses. The authorities remained silent as she called for total destruction of the university as a tool of capitalist society. It was only when Mrs. Miller announced that she would henceforth grant full credit to all students whether they passed their exams or not that the Ministry of Education decided to intervene.

The current trend to expand the horizons of individual freedom and to strengthen the basis of human rights shows no signs of abating. Just one recent edition of the Sunday *New York Times*, that of July 5, 1970, contained the following items in its news section:

—Leading Italian newspapers were demanding increased rights for defendants in criminal cases.
—A federal court had decided in favor of a NYC welfare mother in her suit to get city and state departments of social service to pay all tuition and registration fees for her to study to become a nurse.
—A new law had been enacted in Germany which gave unmarried mothers automatic custody of their children (previously, juvenile authorities had had the last word).
—The governor of Michigan had signed into law a bill giving any citizen the right to sue a public agency or a private industry for fouling the environment. The law's author said "every man in effect would become an attorney general as far as the environment is concerned."
—A new bail reform law was signed by the governor of Massachusetts giving all defendants, except those in capital cases, the right to an early hearing on the right to release on recognizance without putting up bail.
—Japanese women were found to be increasingly taking the initiative in divorce proceedings thanks to their country's new liberal divorce laws.

No, the administrative state does not seem to be ushering in a long night of the human spirit. Rather it seems to be expanding the frontiers of human development and initiative. And it seems likely to keep on doing so. Innovation, specialization, education, and the rest of the now familiar litany of changes which the administrative revolution is causing can only move man farther along the same path. The growth of affluence and leisure, which Disraeli called the two great civilizers of man, can only speed this process.

In his provocative 1967 study of an English country village which he called *Akenfield*, Ronald Blythe records an 85-year-old resident commenting on the changes which had occurred during his working lifetime.

I had to accept everything my governor said to me. I learnt never to answer a word. I dursn't say nothing. Today you can be a man with men, but not then. That is how it was. It will never be like that again.

7

SHELTER WITHOUT WALLS

Men come together in groups and things start to happen—to them. In forming an organization, they set in motion a process long perceived and long utilized by administrators of whatever stripe. This is the process of group identification. Organizations often try to cultivate such identification, hoping thereby to inculcate in their members a spirit of allegiance and sacrifice.

Organizations build this identity in various ways. Rituals, uniforms, songs, mottos, and codes of conduct are only some of the more obvious devices. Most of the activities an organization undertakes and most of the services it provides for its members play some part in making these members think of themselves as components of a formal group. To the extent that the organization meets the individual's financial, professional, and, particularly, his emotional needs, the more likely it is to develop in him a sense of organizational loyalty. And, it has customarily been thought that the more completely an organization can accomplish this, the more effective and efficient it becomes. Words like "morale" and *esprit de corps* are often used to designate the benefits that presumably flow from such a merger of individual and group identity. And "morale" and *esprit de corps* are often regarded as an elixir for organizational health and heartiness.

Administrative theorists have long called attention to this phenomenon and to the ways in which it works. Max Weber pointed out that in providing a group identity for their members organizations gain their loyalty, control their actions, and socialize them into a culture. Anthony Downs takes this theme and goes further, noting that bureaus sometimes even create actual ideologies to strengthen their cohesiveness, fortify their position, and prolong their existence. An organization's success has often been measured by the extent to which it induces its members to think of themselves in *its* terms and to shape their attitudes and their actions to *its* needs.

Such a process has often created problems for the society in which the organization lives and functions. To the extent that the organization instills group loyalty in its members, it tends to set up a wall around itself which makes it less aware of, and less responsive to, the society it is supposed to serve. The more it builds self-identification, the more it becomes isolated from the main currents of the social stream. As Kenneth E. Boulding noted in *The Organizational Revolution,* "the fact that the individual is serving *some* group which is greater than himself blinds him to the fact that his group is only a part of the whole."

As should be obvious, the development of organizational solidarity can, and often does, have adverse effects on the larger society. An organization concerned with its own survival and growth may work at cross-purposes with the social system in which it operates. It may set goals which clash with society's goals. It may engage in bureaucratic warfare with other organizations and so waste resources and impede developments that society needs. It may persist in functioning long after it has actually become dysfunctional. The bureaucratic landscape is dotted with agencies which no longer serve any useful purpose and which may even frustrate the attainment of society's purposes. Yet such agencies can often cling to life with a formidable tenacity when confronted by possible extinction. President Nixon learned this lesson when he sought, in vain, to abolish the United States Government's Board of Tea Tasters in early 1970. The same year, Italy, in reorganizing its bureaucracy, found a public agency busily functioning that was solely devoted to avoiding veterans of the Garibaldi campaigns—the last such campaign had been fought in 1869.

If we look a little further, we find another and somewhat surprising aspect to this phenomenon of organizational identification and solidarity. While the cultivation of such identity may help a threatened organization stay in existence, it doesn't necessarily help it to operate more efficiently. As a matter of fact, the prized organizational values of "morale" and *esprit de corps* can often prove as counterproductive for the organization itself as for society. And this is increasingly true for organizations in these revolutionary times.

As we have already noted, organizational identification tends to produce organizational isolation. The more the organization and its members acquire a heightened awareness of themselves, the more they stand apart from others. The very symbols that are often brought into play, such as uniforms, ceremonies, and codes serve to distinguish the members from their fellow citizens and give them a sense of apartness. A group in isolation, however, often tends to develop unhealthy and unfruitful behavioral patterns within its own structure. The unity which arises may be an artificial one which, strange as it may seem, may only generate more discord and distrust within the organization's own ranks than would otherwise have been the case.

Anyone who has studied the American police closely has been struck by the appearance of two seemingly conflicting tendencies. One is the bond of cohesion which seems to characterize policemen and which results from their isolation from society. The other is the intense intra-organizational bitterness and rancor which often builds up within any police force. American policemen will often go to great lengths to protect and cover up for one another. At the same time, a remarkable degree of distrust and suspicion is found in their relations with one another. As sociologist William Westley has pointed out, the "secrecy code," that is the code of mutual protectiveness, found in American police forces "does not produce a sense of trust. In fact it seems clear that an unauthorized consequence of the emphasis on secrecy is that the police are intensely suspicious of each other."

The same seems to hold true for other highly distinct groups as well. Military organizations and religious orders, while they present a common front of great unity to the outside world, are often seething cauldrons of conflict underneath. Minority groups which have been discriminated against frequently exhibit the same diverse tendencies. While they often act with seeming cohesion in their relations with the majority, they are often at the same time choked with hostility and hatred within their own ranks. When Jews were actively and openly discriminated against in the United States they usually kept closely together and sought to speak, if not with a common voice, then at least with voices that were in harmony. Yet, anyone who was acquainted with Jewish life during those times knows that intense rivalries and animosities were bubbling beneath this veneer of solidarity. Careful observers have spotted the same forces at work in the American Negro community today. In an isolated group, tensions and pressures get dammed up and fail to receive the dissipation which a more open situation would provide.

Needless to say, such feelings as these do not often make for organizational efficiency. And anyone who is familiar with closed-in organizations has come to realize this. Resources are wasted, energies are sacrificed, and efforts are sabotaged. Thus because of the isolation which it fosters, and because this isolation tends to build up internal pressures, the overly cohesive organization is not only not all that cohesive but it is also not all that efficient.

Another factor stemming from the isolation which too much group identification can produce may impair an organization's efficiency even more. When an organization gains a sense of distinctiveness, it tends to lose its sense of perspective. It starts to view its own operations uncritically and blame its problems on other groups. Its relative insulation from such groups discourages the receipt of new ideas from outside itself. Organizations which build thick walls around themselves suffer from a lack of ventilation and from the stifling effects which such a lack can produce.

In describing the rather infamous Court of Chancery of his day, Charles Dickens noted that "the evil of it is that it is a world wrapped up in too much jeweler's cotton and fine wool, and cannot hear the rushing of the larger world . . . it is a deadened world and its growth is sometimes unhealthy for that want of air."

Recent writers on administration have made the same point. In his study of the Forest Service, Herbert Kaufman pointed out that, "an individual imbued with the spirit of an organization, indoctrined with its values, committed to its established goals and customary ways, and dedicated to its traditions, is not likely to experiment a great deal, nor even to see the possibilities suggested by unplanned developments." *

Thus because it slows down innovation and change and because it builds up internal pressures and tensions, an overdose of organizational identification can prove damaging to the organization itself as well as to the larger community it serves. Fortunately for both, such feelings of heightened solidarity are passing from the organizational scene. The administrative revolution is transforming organizations in such a way as to riddle their walls with holes and open them up to the broader influences of society. Organizations both public and private are experiencing less and less ability to isolate themselves from society's main

---

* Some anthropologists claim that it was the need to form links outside the primary organization structure of the family which first led man to establish incest taboos. Exogamy is viewed as necessary to the familial tribe's very survival.

currents. At the same time, they are finding themselves more and more in step with the social forces of their time and are becoming more and more disposed to making their procedures and goals consistent with those of the community in which they exist. The trend is a hesitant and halting one, to be sure, and its progress has certainly been far from uniform. In short, it is only a trend. But it does exist and it is gaining ground all the time.

Planned Program Budgeting System (PPBS), to take one example, forces organizations to think of the total environment. Its emphasis on what the social effect of organizational activities will be, and its stress on external costs and external benefits, forces organizations to think beyond themselves. They must now weigh the consequences of their acts in terms of other organizations and of society. The traditional battle which public organizations frequently, even usually, have waged to promote themselves and their programs at almost any costs to others is, to be sure, not eliminated; but it is altered. Organizations that now wish to increase their activities or even to maintain their existing operations must seek to do so on the basis of the social worth of such activities and their contributions to the overall picture.

Clientele involvement is another factor which is puncturing the organizational wall. As clients continue to cross the organization's threshold, they inject into it a new breath of air and a new breadth of perspective. They tend to disrupt its self-satisfying routines and force it to create linkages with the larger society.

The clientele involvement movement, it is well to note, does not stop with clients alone. It is becoming increasingly the custom for public agencies of all kinds to call on outsiders of all kinds for help and support. In New York City, over 32,000 volunteers were working without pay for public agencies at the beginning of 1970. This figure represented a more than 200 percent increase since the city established its Volunteer Coordinating Council three years before. These volunteers were donating a minimum of four hours a week patrolling the streets and housing projects as auxiliary policemen, aiding libraries and hospitals, maintaining athletic fields, and caring for the aged.

Even organizations hitherto considered somewhat sacrosanct are starting to open their doors to outside participants. Among this group are the courts. The Boulder County Juvenile Court of Colorado began using volunteers in 1961. They not only have helped to set up and operate extensive tutoring programs but they are now working at medical, psychological, and other tasks depending on their skills. The movement has caught on and spread. By the end of the decade such volunteer court programs had been launched or were in the process of being launched in 45 states plus a number of foreign countries.

Another aspect of the administrative revolution which is tearings gaps in organizational fences is specialization. MacGregor once noted that the personnel needs of organizations would become much less predictable in the future, making it necessary to have "a heterogeneous supply of human resources from which individuals can be selected to fill a variety of specific but unpredictable needs." The future which Mac-Gregor foresaw has now arrived, and today organizations are reaching outside their boarders to take advantage of a gamut of specialists and specialized services.

One way in which this shows itself is in the ever increasing use of consultants. By bringing in outside consultants for brief periods of time, organizations are able to take advantage of specialized skills which they may not need and could not provide on a full-time, year-round basis. The practice has been decried by some like former Avis Rent-a-Car president Robert Townsend who claims a consultant is someone who borrows your watch to tell you what time it is and then walks off with it. But the practice is growing all the time in both business and government.

The value of the consultant, it should be emphasized, does not lie in his special skills alone but also in his perspective. As an outsider he can view the organization and its operations in a more detached and objective manner. Furthermore, being outside the stream of daily organizational activity, he enjoys blocks of time necessary to think through some of the organization's more fundamental and troublesome problems. "Consultants are not hit by the routine of daily operations that city workers and administrators must fight to get through," says Fred O. R. Hayes, Budget Director for the city of New York, an organization which, despite its huge size, still makes heavy use of such outside skills. "You can have people as sharp inside government," notes Hayes, "but there's always some chief administrator's speech to be written or a hundred other problems that come up to sidetrack the specialist from his task."

Increasingly, organizations are starting to farm out even portions of their regular operations to other organizations. Such vital internal activities as payroll, inventory, security, training, recruiting, etc., are more and more being placed in the hands of external agencies. Banks, for one, are taking on much of this work for their clients, while the banks themselves are frequently turning over most of their electronic data processing operations to another outside organization to handle. As might be expected, this trend has advanced much further and faster in the private than in the public sector, although the latter has, if anything, even more to gain. (I know of one regional agency of the federal government which is being charged $2,000 a year by its parent organization to make up its payroll; the agency could have a local bank perform this chore for $15 a week. The California Insurance Fund, it will be recalled, has allowed its field offices to contract for staff services with private firms, if it can do so at less of a cost than that charged by the Fund's own staff units.)

Even the specialization which is going on within the organization itself tends to dissolve the organization's solidarity. A community of experience has long been recognized by administrative theorists as a primary force in building organizational cohesion. But with the organization's members becoming increasingly specialized, such common experiences are tending to diminish in number and intensity.

The two features which accompany specialization, professionalization and education, are also eroding organizational insularity. Professionalization tends to create a work force that is more loyal to the goals and standards of the various professions and thereby less obeisant to the goals and standards of the organization itself. "In a fluid organizational setting, and in an economy of tight labor markets," said General Electric's "Report on Our Future Business Environment," "it will become progressively easier for an individual to consider his prime commitment to be his profession and/or his self-development, not to a single organization."

Aiding and abetting this tendency is the well-known wanderlust which frequently grips knowledge workers. They tend to pass in and out of organizations much more easily than other employees. Often, they seem not only ready but eager to cut their organizational ties when a new opportunity or simply a new challenge offers itself. All it frequently takes is an ungrazed and not necessarily greener pasture to lure them on. Furthermore, as Peter Drucker has noted, knowledge workers tend to get bored even with their own knowledge in 20 years or so and consequently strike out not just for new challenges in their own line of work but even for new lines of work themselves. Career changes at mid-career are becoming a more and more visible part of the organizational scene.

The growing emphasis on continuous, on-going education also shakes up the organization and its members. Often, the acquisition of such training takes the members outside the organization itself and puts them in classrooms with members of other groups. They return to their own organizational setting with new ideas and new perspectives. The personal contacts they make will also decrease the isolation of the organization they serve. In some organizations, such as the police, the schools, the military, etc., it is often customary for the members to spend much if not most of their leisure time associating with one another. This normally reinforces organizational in-group tendencies. However, education, along with the other features of the administrative revolution which we have noted, tends to reduce this drastically.

A further factor which we have not yet directly pinpointed but which is nevertheless a part of the administrative revolution is also undermining the sacred canons of organizational solidarity. This is the rising trend toward what is sometimes called "representativeness."

At one time, many organizations tended to recruit their members from particular social, ethnic, or religious groups. Membership positions in the diplomatic corps, for example, were frequently reserved for members of the upper-classes. Other classes or social groups were used for other organizations or for certain ranges of activities within these organizations. Police forces tended to recruit from rural areas in England and France and, in the latter country, more particularly from Corsica. In this country, the Irish have tended to dominate the police while white Southerners have frequently been predominant in the Army. The "capture" of an agency by a particular social, ethnic, or even geographic group may occur by design or by chance reinforced by habit. In any case, however, it adds to the membership's community of experience, a force which as we have already seen makes for organizational cohesion.

The modern organization is increasingly less likely to be a captive of any particular group. In many countries, governments have taken specific steps to broaden the recruitment bases for their organizations. Although members of the working class are still not represented in the upper echelons of any country's administrative apparatus in proportion to their numbers, they are more in evidence today than ever before. And their proportions are steadily rising. The increased mobility and fluidity of modern society, and the high employment rates it usually maintains, combined with the growing insistence of equal opportunity, further erodes the possibility for any group to make any organization into a fiefdom for its own members.

Such political scientists as Norton Long and Peter Woll point out that the federal bureaucracy is already more representative of the United States population than is the membership of Congress. The same characteristics appear to be true in many other countries as well. Needless to add, most writers on administration welcome this change. As Long puts it, "representativeness must be a prime consideration in the recruitment process."

A further aspect of this trend toward "representativeness" is the disintegration of sexual barriers, both formal and informal, in organizational personnel policies. At one time, the military, the police, the clergy, and other groups were restricted to males. Now women are increasingly swelling their ranks. At one time such fields as primary education, social work, and nursing were dominated, at least in this country, by women. In nursing, the domination was virtually complete. Today, more and more men are entering these and other hitherto feminine sanctuaries. The community of experience within the organization's membership thus suffers another setback and so does its self-contained solidarity.

One final factor of the technological age is also causing organizational walls to dissolve: the growing interdependence of skills and knowledge. Computers and data storage banks lead easily, almost automatically, to information exchanges that cross organizational lines. Adding pressure to this push is the growing need for knowledge of all kinds. "Previously isolated bureaus," writes Ida R. Hoos, "when locked into the larger systems will have to adjust the pace of their activities to be consistent with the rest. Even the rugged individualist administrator who resists entangling alliances may be forced to acquiesce for whatever his province, he is facing a mass of data increasing at such a rate that record keeping by present methods will soon require more personnel than the tax base can support."

One of the reasons why the need for information is increasing is the growing recognition that problems are multidimensional and cannot always be solved with an attack on just one front. The welfare organization cannot solve welfare problems without working with labor, schools, and other organizations. The police cannot solve crime problems by concentrating on simple law enforcement. The business firm cannot produce efficiently unless the universities supply it with members equipped with requisite skills and the community supplies the requisite facilities.

Areas of knowledge themselves are growing less and less demarcated. The distinction between organic and inorganic chemistry is blurring, notes Peter Drucker, and both are becoming increasingly involved with physics and biology. Psychology and physiology are increasingly inter-related while psychology is also stepping on the toes of philosophy and religion. The various branches of social science are actually becoming indistinguishable from each other, although many academic departments refuse to accept this fact. And all of them are making increased use of mathematics.

The growing interdependence between areas of knowledge and the growing interrelatedness of problems is changing administration in a variety of ways. The interdepartmental committee, once a largely British device, is becoming a fixture in the administrative apparatus of most countries. President Nixon has revived the long neglected device of the Cabinet meeting so that his department heads can exchange ideas and gain acquaintance with what their colleagues are doing. Such mayors as John Lindsay of New York and Kevin White of Boston are doing the same thing.

At lower levels a vast proliferation of committees, task forces, and what-have-you have blossomed and though their concrete results are not always immediately impressive, their impact on organizational life is nevertheless growing. The modern world allows few organizations the chance to wrap themselves into cocoons and remain oblivious to what is going on around them. The present day organization, far from being an enclosed enclave, is more of a coordinating nexus and its activities tend to become increasingly involved with, and thus increasingly attuned to, the society it serves.

OPENING THE ORGANIZATION: THE PUBLIC SECTOR

We need undertake no long march through the corridors of bureaucracy to find examples of this wall-puncturing trend at work. Organizations undergoing the opening up process exist everywhere and more of them are coming into existence all the time. Even public agencies which have hitherto maintained a fairly strict aloofness from involvements with other organizations or with the broader forces of society are feeling and showing its effects. Sometimes the process is painful; sometimes it is pleasant. Almost invariably, it is salutary for all concerned.

One such organization which is crawling out of, or being pulled from, its protective shell is the public school. In the United States, educational institutions have enjoyed a fair degree of immunity from the normal processes of government. They have come to regard themselves, and to be regarded by many others, as a sort of holy ground which the citizenry may enter only at special times and for designated, largely spectator, purposes. All that is now changing.

One of the first instances of such a shift was the development of the community school. Pioneered in New Haven, Connecticut during the late 1950s and since adopted elsewhere, the community school regards itself as an institution for the entire community or at least the entire neighborhood. It stays open during the evening hours and frequently during weekends to play host to, and even to sponsor, a variety of community events. One of Boston's elementary schools will soon provide housing, recreation, medical, and other social services in addition to education, all in one building. The concept of the school as an all-purpose institution has been welcomed by some educators, opposed by others, but, at all events, it appears to have taken root in many localities and shows no signs of fading away.

Still more significant perhaps in the field of educational organization is the emergence of the "school without walls." Heeding Plato's admonition that "the city educates," Philadelphia inaugurated its Parkway Program in 1969. The Parkway classes meet in dozens of locations throughout the city—in churches, museums, insurance companies, etc. The concept has been judged a huge success by educators, parents, and students. Starting with 142 students, it had reached 700 by June 1970, and thousands of other student applications had been turned down. The program has started to catch fire in other cities. In September 1970, Boston was scheduled to open a downtown high school expressly designed to bring its young people into everyday contact with the facts of everyday urban life.

Another long insulated organization which is succumbing to the wall-dissolving trend is the mental hospital. In his book *Asylums*, Irving Goffman concluded that such institutions often end up being run primarily for the benefit of their own staff. This is an indication of the degree to which they had become self-contained and self-serving. But all that is beginning to change. For one thing, they are in part being supplemented by community mental health centers which treat patients living in the community or, in some cases, in half-way houses. These mental health centers work, in turn, with the mental hospitals and, in so doing, help to breach the latter's organizational walls. The volunteer movement has also engulfed such hospitals, creating new links between them and the outside world. And PPBS is starting to have its impact on them as well.

Traditionally, the police have been the most isolated group of public servants in the civilian community. Their uniforms and weapons, their largely repressive tasks, and even their odd hours have often made them something of a state within a state. All too often, the police station has stood as an embattled fortress within the neighborhood it serves. But police stations are starting to open their doors. This trend is particularly advanced in many European countries where police departments frequently use their own facilities for bicycle clinics, traffic kindergartens (where young children are allowed to ride model cars and thereby learn the rules of the road), and other activities. However, the trend is also starting to catch hold in the United States as well. Some police stations today are offering advice to persons needing various kinds of assistance and are providing meeting rooms, not only for their community relations boards but for other events not directly connected with police work. Police departments are also employing computer specialists, planning experts, attorneys, community relations specialists, and others from the civilian sector.

Finally, the most isolated and, frequently the most troublesome of all arms of government, the military, is also loosening up the tightly knit structure in which it has so long enfolded its members. The United States Naval Academy now has a faculty that is 50 percent civilian. Its counterpart at West Point still uses only Army officers but it requires them to have Ph.D.'s from civilian institutions if they wish to gain promotion to the rank of associate or full professor. Cadets at West Point can now spend as much as 55 percent of their time studying social sciences and the humanities, and each cadet receives a free copy of the *New York Times* every day. As a result of such measures, we have had such developments as the Concerned Officers Movement, an organization of military officers who oppose the Vietnam war.

It is in Israel, however, where we find the most dramatic example of an opened-up military establishment. Nearly all able-bodied citizens up to the age of 49 have some involvement with the country's armed forces. When a professional dance troupe called "The New Music Hall of Israel" toured the United States in 1969 reporters found that nearly all the male dancers were reservists in their country's paratroop corps while the troupe's 39-year-old choreographer, a former dancer himself, held a reserve commission in the artillery. Women not only serve in the reserves but make up one-third of the regular Israeli army.

The openness of the Israeli military structure is fostered still further by mingling the reservists with the regulars when on duty. For example, NBC in a report on the Israeli air force in 1970, noted that 8 of 12 planes which had executed a recent afternoon bombing raid over Egypt had been piloted by reservists. These eight reservists had spent the morning at their civilian jobs and were back at those same jobs the following morning. The Israeli military, it should further be noted, maintains no hospitals of its own. It sends its wounded to civilian hospitals so that they will feel less lonely and isolated. Through such steps as these Israel has produced a defense establishment that is more efficient and less costly, as well as one that is much less dominated by the military mystique.

Turning to Europe we find several moves afoot to open up public service organizations to the outside world. Great Britain appointed a royal commission in 1966 to study the civil service. Known as the Fulton Commission, it issued a report in 1968 stating, among other things, that the civil service had become too isolated from the community at large. It recommended late entry and transferable pension schemes as ways of promoting mobility between the service and outside employment. It also urged the engagement of outside specialists on short-terms contracts.

The German government has already begun to put into effect a reorganization which will open up its bureaucracy to some freshening currents from the larger society. It requires federal agencies to use outside specialists and outside services to improve their efficiency. France now allows its civil servants the right to take leaves of absence for up to five years in order to take jobs in teaching or in private enterprise. Furthermore, third year students at the government's Academy of Administration now receive training in private business management and sometimes are given internships in commercial enterprises.

In Sweden, meanwhile, the trend toward greater intermingling between public and private agencies is already far advanced. All Swedish departments have ministerial advisors known as State Secretaries. According to Brian Chapman, nearly 80 percent of these posts were filled by civil servants in the 1920–40 period. By 1949, the proportion of civil servants holding these positions had dropped to 50 percent; five years later it had declined to 40 percent. Filling the places of the departing civil servants have been men and women from labor, academe, industry, and the mass media. Sweden also has long had a policy of turning over to various interest groups actual governmental functions for them to administer under government supervision.

These new trends in the public sector have prompted a member of the Canadian Senate, Maurice LaMontagne, to speculate on the future of public officials. He maintains that the increasing invasion of the public services by the intellectual and commercial communities, the rising number of royal commissions, task forces, and advisory boards and councils, and the growing use of public opinion polls are working to bring about what he calls "the twilight of the civil servants."

In this country, former Civil Service Commission chairman John Macey, Jr. sees these changes in a somewhat different light. Rather than being predictive of a bureaucratic *Götterdämmerung*, he views them as leading to the development of a new and much more desirable type of public employee. In dedicating the Federal Executive Institute in Charlottesville, Virginia in late 1968, Macey depicted the federal executive of the future as being more broadly educated and much more mobile, rising up the career ladder by working in various agencies and in various positions. As a result, said Macey, he will be less committed to a parent organization and "more committed to a specific public policy, regardless of where he may be working at a given period of time."

OPENING THE ORGANIZATION: THE PRIVATE SECTOR

If the administrative revolution is opening the doors and windows of public organizations, then it is nearly razing the beams and pillars of many private ones. The same wall-dissolving forces and trends which we have seen affecting government are affecting business with an even greater impact.

The issue of employee mobility is a case in point. While government organizations are seeking to encourage more circulation of their memberships, many business organizations are starting to resemble railroad terminals where employees merely spend time before taking off for some place else. This is particularly true when it comes to knowledge workers. What is intriguing in this new revolving-door trend is that many sectors of business are actually encouraging it. At one time, the job-hopper found himself at an increasing disadvantage in making his way up the ladder of business success. Now, he finds the tables turned in his favor. From being something of a pariah, he has become something of a hero. This is especially true in the modern and fastest growing sectors of business. A friend of mine who spent eight years as a sales manager for a small electronics firm and then decided to strike out for fresh territory found it impossible to do so. The fact that he had stayed on so many years with one firm made other prospective employers suspicious of him.

Eugene E. Jennings, a professor at Michigan State University's School of Business, points out that there is an increasing correlation between job mobility and job success in the business world. Top level executives are increasingly coming from the ranks of those who spent their working lives not with one organization but with several. Within the organization itself, the new executive has usually worked in various subunits before making his way to the upper echelon. Jennings calls this new type of organization member "mobicentric man" and, he says, "mobicentric man" is replacing the Insider and the Organization Toady with increasing rapidity.

When it comes to constructing interrelationships with outside organizations, the business organization is also far ahead of the public one. It is parcelling out a mounting proportion of its operations to other firms. Some commercial companies have even started to use outside assistance to help them "dehire," that is, get rid of someone whom they no longer need or want. Outside employment specialists are brought in to help the dismissed employee prepare himself for, and obtain, a job somewhere else. In July 1970, the *Wall Street Journal* reported that a growing number of employment firms were taking on such assignments.

To accommodate themselves to the growing complexity and rapid rate of innovation in modern technology, business firms are dispatching employees to the campus and schoolhouse with rising frequency. IBM has even sent employees through four years of medical school on a full-time basis so that it could utilize their talents to the fullest in developing new equipment for medical technology. Executives, junior and senior, are frequently sent to university settings for special seminars lasting a few hours, a few days, or even weeks. The purpose of the seminars often is not to develop special skills but to stimulate their minds and expand their perspectives.

When it comes to "mind-blowing" experiences, business organizations are often showing quite a bit of tolerance and even verve. For example, the National Security Industrial Association, an organization of munitions makers, invited radical writer Paul Goodman to speak at their 1967 meeting. Goodman accepted the invitation, showed up, and promptly proceded to denounce his hosts as un-American, as being a major factor in causing the Newark, New Jersey riots of that year, and as being "the most dangerous body of men at present in the world." He received polite though restrained applause. The San Francisco Chamber of Commerce received a similar though somewhat more earthy scorching when they invited Black Panther leader Eldridge Cleaver to address one of their get-togethers.

The growth of citizen response to social problems is also breaking down corporate insularity. As publicly-owned corporations increasingly replace private ones, and as stock ownership becomes ever more widely diffused in the hands of more and more individuals—already one in four adults in the United States own publicly traded stocks—business finds itself increasingly vulnerable to all sorts of outside pressures. Eastman Kodak, for example, found itself forced to yield to pressures by churches and other socially conscious institutions and individuals among its stockholders and do more in the field of minority employment. In 1970, General Motors became the target of a concerted drive by consumer interests to name three consumer representatives to its Board of Directors. *Campaign* GM, as it was called, failed but it may have provided some writing on the wall. GM and other corporations will undoubtedly continue to feel its effects. The modern corporation, particularly if it is a large one, operates in a wide arena with not only a high visibility but also with many points of entrance into and out of the audience.

"The corporation," wrote Adolph A. Berle, Jr. in 1954, "is now essentially a non-statist political institution, and its directors are in the same boat with public office holders." This finding is gaining validity as the public corporation finds its boat increasingly rocked by the same waves which are ruffling the waters of nearly all social institutions at the present time.

The public sector itself is helping to open up the private sector in a variety of ways. The stepped-up regulatory efforts by government are forcing modern business to unlock its books, divulge its activities, and increase its general pattern of external relationships. What is adding thrust to this growing interrelationship between private and public organizations is the growing realization by each that the other is not necessarily the enemy. When government regulates, its effect on business has often, in the long run at least, been benign. Most stock market executives, for example, concede that government regulation of the securities market has actually been a boon since it has resulted in a more orderly operation and has built public confidence in the industry. Much of the consumer legislation that has been passed, including truth-in-lending laws, though opposed by business at the time, appears to be having similar beneficial effects.

A much stronger force that is producing an interpenetration between public and private organizations is the rise in government spending. Accompanying this rise is the growing trend on the part of many government agencies, particularly newer ones, to spend more of their money by giving it out to other institutions. While this brings in revenue to business firms, it also brings in the civil servants to arrange, inspect, and sometimes supervise. Many would be surprised to see the way even a large corporation will often grovel at the feet of a $14,000-a-year government official who has arrived to check up on just how the firm is doing on its government contract. (And the more cynical might be suprised to see how strict and ethical such government officials usually are.)

As might be expected, it has been the advent of government economic planning which has perhaps had the most drastic effect in cracking open business organizations. For example, French business executives, long obsessed with the notion of secretiveness, find themselves increasingly forced to divulge their secrets to government and to other representatives of the economy. As government everywhere intervenes more and more into the commercial affairs of the nations they govern, they divest these commercial institutions of their long-prized privacy. Going a step further, we find that in many countries, government is actually becoming a partner to business in many commercial and quasi-commercial enterprises. Italy has two government agencies continually purchasing stock in private firms for the express purpose of forcing such firms to streamline their organizational structure, modernize their business practices, or simply adopt more socially oriented business policies. The Swedish government in 1969 bought a controlling interest in the nation's drug producing industries for the same purpose. KLM, the innovative Dutch airline whose stock is publicly traded on the New

York and Amsterdam exchanges, is half-owned by the Dutch government. In this country, the federal government is partners with business firms in Comsat, the Communications Satellite Corporation.

But perhaps the most significant trend which is bringing business policies more in line with national priorities is simply the fact that in a welfare state, the interests of both tend to converge. This trend is difficult for many to accept and certainly exceptions to it abound. Yet the evidence is mounting that what is good for the nation *increasingly tends* to be good for business and vice versa.

A brief look at two of America's most pressing problems as this is being written, the Vietnam War and domestic poverty, will show how this works. Business profits increased steadily and markedly during the first half of the 1960s as the so-called New Economics began to take hold. With our accelerated involvement in the war in 1965, this trend started to disintegrate. Business profits began to falter while inflation roared ahead. As a result, Robert Eisner, Professor of Economics at Northwestern University, calculated early in 1970 that real, that is, adjusted-for-inflation business profits had dropped 16.8 percent since the Vietnam buildup began. This was more than eight times the 2 percent dip in real worker wages which occurred during the same time.

My own studies indicate that the defense suppliers themselves experienced losses which not only equalled but even exceeded those suffered by business as a whole. Working under fixed price contracts which could not be adjusted for inflation, and subject to other pressures as well, most of the large Pentagon contractors actually earned less in 1969 than they did in 1965 *without even adjusting for the inflationary dollar*. One of the Big Five defense contractors, Douglas Aircraft, was forced to the financial wall in 1967 while a second Big Five contractor, Lockheed, was teetering on the verge of bankruptcy as 1970 got under way.

Poverty in a welfare state becomes particularly burdensome for everyone, not least of all for business. In every major city in the United States at the present time, the slums are providing the least per capita revenue and are consuming the most in terms of per capita expenditures. Health services, education services, fire services, etc., must all be supplied to the slum dweller at a cost far exceeding that given to the nonpoor. My own examination of the New York City budget indicates that if the city could accommodate its poor citizens with the same amount of expenditures which it disburses for its middle- and upper-income citizens, then the New York City budget could be cut in half. The situation in other cities is similar.

What is true for cities is generally true for states and the federal government. The poor contribute the least and cost the most. When one adds in the loss to the nation's productive capacity and purchasing power through poverty, and the price of the external social costs which poverty breeds, such as facilities for prosecuting and incarcerating the disproportionate number of criminal offenders which come from the slums, the dollar costs of poverty mount still higher. One sees vividly the accuracy of Gunnar Myrdal's statement that the rest of the American people would live better, not worse, if poverty were to be eliminated. And one doesn't have to attribute any higher motives than simple corporate greed to the increasing desire which businessmen are manifesting to bring about such an end.

This new trend is producing some unusual alliances and making for some strange bedfellows. When Governor George Romney called the Michigan Legislature into special session in the fall of 1967 to pass a package of civil rights bills, the lobbyists for the big auto companies immediately sprang into action. They urged and exhorted legislators so feverishly to vote for the bills that some legislators began to refer to Stewart Didzum and Hyram Todd, lobbyists for Ford and Chrysler, as "Rap" Didzum and "Stokeley" Todd. The Detroit Free Press made the following comment: "Where in the past big business may have given encouragement and support to civil rights leaders trying to eliminate discrimination through legislative means, now big business itself presses and demands laws. It is the driving force."

Of course, there are still many issues that divide the interests of particular business organizations or groups of business organizations from those of society. But, here too, a new business institution is emerging which promises to reduce, though by no means eliminate, these divergences. This is the multipurpose corporation.

THE MULTIPURPOSE CORPORATION

Textiles have long been the sick old man of the American economy. In a sense, the industry has never recovered from the Great Depression. What has principally ailed the textile industry and continues to afflict it is the fact that it uses comparatively large amounts of labor and comparatively low amounts of capital in manufacturing its products. Since labor is relatively expensive in the United States compared with other lands, while capital is not, the American textile industry has suffered and suffered greatly from foreign competition. What vigor it still retains is to a great extent due to the protective tariffs and import controls with which the United States government has shielded it. The stocks of some textile companies sell for less today than they did during the 1920s.

However, two textile companies have, to a considerable extent, escaped the dismal fate of their fellows. These are Textron Incorporated and Indian Head. In a period when their colleagues were shrivelling up and falling by the wayside, these two companies managed to forge ahead.

Why?

The answer is essentially a simple one. They diversified. Indian Head now has 22 divisions making glass containers and automotive accessories in addition to various textile products. Textron boasts 33 divisions which turn out aerospace products, saws, watchbands, pens, snowmobiles, auto-body parts, etc.

Diversification has not been confined to textile concerns. It has become a growing practice throughout the American industrial scene. More and more corporations have taken to performing more and more varied and oftentimes completely unrelated tasks. Even such stodgy giants as U.S. Steel and Inland Steel have bolted their fences to graze in other pastures. The former has been making inroads into general aviation; the latter has become involved in the computer software business. The multipurpose concept is alive, well, and growing.

This trend toward diversification should not be confused with the conglomerate craze which blossomed in the United States during the mid-1960s and, for a few years, enjoyed some dizzying speculative successes before being brought to the ground. The conglomerate fad, which saw a few voracious entrepreneurial corporations gobbling up others at a furious rate, was based largely on financial manipulation. Through the use of dubious accounting practices, plus some loopholes in the tax laws, and helped by a buoyant stock market, these conglomerates grew and seemed to prosper until the bear market, new SEC regulations, new accounting principles, and their own speculative excesses punctured their overinflated balloons. But while the conglomerate craze is now, hopefully, fading from the scene, the diversification movement continues apace.

Since even the soundest diversification effort usually involves some corporate mergers and takeovers, many see in this trend a new form of corporate cannibalism that will only lead to greater monopoly and control of the American economy. Such fears, however, lack justification. Even in 1968, when the conglomerate craze was at its height, the total number of companies listed on all the major stock exchanges increased. In other words, there were more than enough up-and-coming companies to take the places of those that had been taken over. As a matter of fact, there are more separate businesses in the United States today *in proportion to population* than there were in 1900. And such giants as U.S. Steel, ALCOA and Du Pont control a much smaller proportion of their markets today than they did a generation ago. Du Pont, as a matter of fact, is having a difficult time holding on to a mere 8 percent of the domestic chemical market. The most consolidation is found in the auto industry where the big three, or, with American Motors, three and one-half still control all domestic auto production. But foreign sales are increasingly eating away at their customer base, such sales having reached nearly 17 percent of all auto sales in the United States in 1969.

Far from eroding competition in the American economy, the diversification movement actually strengthens it. Small companies finding it difficult to survive in a competitive industry are often saved from extinction by becoming part of a larger firm outside their field. Large companies are encouraged to disperse their energies into several markets rather than concentrating on just one. Providing stockholders with potential opportunities to sell out their ownership to other corporations further catalyzes the competitive forces at work in the American economy and keeps company managements on their toes. The greatest opposition to the merger movement, it is interesting to note, has come from entrenched and sleepy managements of companies that have hitherto enjoyed comparatively stable if not semimonopolistic positions in their particular markets.

The multipurpose concept, it should be stressed, is by no means an exclusively American device. The principle has won wide acceptance in many other industrialized lands, most notably Israel.

The multipurpose corporation has a significant role to play in the administrative revolution. First, it introduces more heterogeneity into the company's structure, operations, and work force, bringing with it all the attendant benefits which we have previously noted. Insularity and isolation are among the first casualties of diversification. In a multi-purpose company, we are likely to find all kinds of employees working at all kinds of tasks in all kinds of places. These employees have much more freedom to diversify their own experiences and foster their own growth than do their colleagues in the single-purpose firm. The problem of the straying scientist which we noticed in Chapter 4 becomes much less acute. A multipurpose company may want to encourage rather than impede a scientist from developing a hot idea which lies outside his area of assignment. If his idea bears fruit, the company can either incorporate it into another division of its activities or establish or acquire such a new division to utilize it.

"In the innovating society," Max Ways has written, "no company can expect to maintain indefinitely a given product line or a given market position or a given technology or a given set of marketing methods or a given set of financial arrangements." The multipurpose company is in step with the modern age and can best bring the administrative benefits of innovation, specialization, and professionalization to fruition.

The greater ability of a diversified company to maintain stability and even growth when one of its products or one of the industries in which it is involved suffers a setback, helps to achieve yet another goal of the administrative revolution, participation. There is a danger in encouraging employees to invest in the company that employs them. What if the company's product line becomes obsolete? Or what if the industry in which it is involved becomes outmoded? The employee who has invested in the company may thereby lose in two ways: his job and his savings. The multipurpose concept alleviates, though it does not remove, this double jeopardy. By spreading its risks and opportunities through a variety of products and markets, the diversified company is less likely to go under or even suffer a crushing blow when one of its products or markets gives out. Consequently, an employee can invest his earnings with somewhat greater assurance that, although setbacks may occur, he is less likely to lose his entire equity.

But the most important, and the most exciting aspect of the multipurpose company lies in its increased attunement to overall social goals. As companies become more diversified they bcome more reflective of the general economy and consequently more oriented to the general welfare. We can see this at work by examining two socially troublesome industries, armaments and cigarettes.

While the major defense suppliers were busily turning out goods for the Vietnam War, they were at the same time increasingly diversifying into more and more civilian operations. Not only their absolute but even the proportional amount of their civilian backlog orders rose rapidly during the war years. For some, such as Boeing and McDonnell-Douglas, this principally took the form of increased civilian plane contracts. Others, however, have proved much more venturesome. AVCO went into the insurance and land development business, Raytheon pioneered in home heating systems, set up a home appliance line, and acquired two publishing firms. United Aircraft, through a subsidiary, developed the turbo-train. By 1970 nearly all the armament makers were feverishly engaged in expanding into the civilian sector and the proportion of their civilian business to their total business was steadily rising. The success of many of their new activities, such as those involved in home construction, home appliances, publishing, etc., directly hinged on the coming of peace.

The cigarette industry provides another illustration of how diversification can make the interest of a problem industry less of a problem to itself and to the larger society. When the anticigarette movement began to gather steam in the early 1960s the cigarette makers marshalled their forces and launched a furious counterattack. They succeeded in first holding up, and then greatly reducing, the thrust of the early legislation requiring them to put a health warning on cigarette packages. But gradually, their opposition to the government's anticigarette activity, while it certainly did not die out, began to assume less of the character of a life and death struggle. The reason is that their existence became less dependent on a continuing high demand for their basic product. R. J. Reynolds, which makes a third of all the cigarettes smoked in the United States, acquired Hawaiian Punch, Chun King Foods and, at last report, was seeking to take over McLean Industries, a large transportation company. Philip Morris became the owners of the American Safety Razor Company, Burma-Vita Company, a shaving firm, and Clark Brothers Chewing Gum Company. The Lorilard Corporation, which produces Old Golds, was itself taken over and is now merely one division of Lowes Theaters Incorporated.

The impact of such trends should not be overstated. Those who make cigarettes still oppose efforts to curb their consumption. Those who make munitions are still ready to bid on Pentagon contracts. Yet, in these and many other industries, the ardor for waging all-out battle is subsiding. A diversified company has not only less need to engage in such a fight but it has less capacity to do so. It simply cannot squander all its resources to protect just one of its operations. It has too many other fish to fry.

As diversification continues to grow, more and more companies which have been pursuing narrow interests with concentrated zeal will have to pursue broader interests with less concentrated zeal. These broader interests will put them more in step with the general economy. And since the general economy of the modern welfare state is highly dependent on the general good, we may expect to see an increasing convergence of interest between the business corporation and the human community.

CORPORATIONS AND COMMUNES:
THE ORGANIZATIONAL COMMUNITY

Revolutions are often exciting to read about but are often unpleasant to experience. Changing times are trying times. Historians and philosophers have long called attention to this fact. As Alfred North Whitehead put it, "the major advances in civilization are processes which all but wreck the societies in which they occur."

Perhaps the greatest wreckage which the recent flood tide of progress has cast up on the beach is our sense of community. This was first noted and poignantly expressed by the sociologist Robert A. Nisbet in his justifiably celebrated work *The Quest for Community*. Man has paid dearly for his breath-taking leap into freedom, Nisbet pointed out, and now he realizes it. "Not the free individual but the lost individual; not independence but isolation; not self-discovery but self-obsession; not to conquer but to be conquered: these are the major states of mind in contemporary imaginative literature," he said.

Underlying this "growing sense of isolation," in Nisbet's view, was the growing realization that the traditional primary relationships of men had become functionally irrelevant and spiritually meaningless. Large organizations had begun taking the place of such institutions as family, neighborhood, and church and he could not visualize these organizations as doing the job which the former institutions had done.

However, Nisbet wrote his book in the early 1950s just as the changes in administration which we have been examining were in the process of being thought out. It is now time to reconsider the whole problem. Can the new administration and the new institutions which it is gradually creating fulfill man's quest for community? Can the administrative revolution replace what the organizational revolution at first destroyed?

To answer this question, we must first dispel a plethora of false images and ideas as to just what communities in the past have been like. When we examine them closely, we see that despite all the misty-eyed nostalgia with which they are nowadays so often described, they rarely if ever provided man with anything resembling a blissful existence.

As noted in Chapter 1 a good deal of the anthropological research which has emerged in recent years shows traditional societies to have been, if anything, more oppressive to the human spirit than our current phase of alienation and anomie. The Pueblo Indians, for instance, were once thought to have found the secret of harmonious togetherness and to have created a near perfect cooperative community. More recent investigation has proved this to be nonsense. The Pueblos, according to anthropologist Peter Farb, are "anxiety-ridden, suspicious, hostile, fearful and ambitious." They bicker endlessly over wives, property, status, etc. And the average Pueblo spends about half his waking hours in religious activities designed to assuage his many fears and tensions.

Another traditional society long considered an idyllic picture of true community have been the Samoans. But, according to anthropologist Henry A. Selby, this isn't true either. Samoans also are deeply immersed in jealousies, rivalries, and hostilities and they often get into voracious and homicidal fights when drinking. They have a rigid and elaborate sense of hierarchy and frequently fake genealogies going back 13 generations in order to acquire increased status. Even their vaunted sexual freedom is more myth than reality, says Selby. Adultery is brutally punished and, in any case, incest taboos are so extensive that it is difficult for the Samoan to find a single mate, much less lead the promiscuous and carefree lovelife so often attributed to him.

As we follow the path of social evolution up to the present time, we fail to find any true models of the type of community that modern man believes he has lost. The medieval city, the European rural village, the small town of early America all fall far short of living up to the glowing pictures so often painted of them. They did provide a sense of community, it is true, but they did so at a fearful cost. Contormity, hierarchy, lack of privacy, and sheer dreariness are only some of the price tags which the sense of community has traditionally borne.

In our quest for community, therefore, we come face to face with a formidable fact: modern man cannot tolerate a community in the traditional sense. He is much too liberated or, if you prefer, much too spoiled. He has become too devoted to such things as independence, privacy, and variety. He requires something quite new. And it might well be that the administrative revolution is tailored to meet his new requirements.

At the outset we should remember that the basis of community is not simple residence but mutual or interrelated activity. Nisbet quotes Ortega y Gasset as pointing out "people do not live together merely to be together. They live together to do something together." Consequently, the modern organization starts out fulfilling the primary community function of joint endeavor. And increasingly, it is doing so in ways which fulfill intellectual and emotional, as well as physical and financial needs.

At the same time, modern organizations are taking on a variety of non-work-related functions that have usually been regarded as community activities. Increasingly organizations are providing such things as medical care, marriage counseling, recreational programs, and education. As for this latter function, it has been estimated that one-third of all the educational programs in the country are now being carried on by work organizations. Arthur D. Little has actually applied to the Massachusetts Board of Higher Education for authority to give masters' degrees in industrial management.

Especially noteworthy is the growing evidence that work organizations are able to provide such community-like services in a highly effective manner. In its survey of company-sponsored alcoholic rehabilitation programs, the *Wall Street Journal* found that the success rate of such programs was 55 to 70 percent higher than those operated by hospitals and clinics. Vocational training programs operated by business corporations have also proven much more successful than those run by Job Corps camps and other institutions. In this case, it is believed that the ability of the trainee to relate his educational experience to his prospective work experience and work setting is one of the main reasons why the corporations have outdone most other agencies in transforming unemployables into employees.

Many organizations are fostering political participation as well. Some business firms now invite candidates from both major parties to address their employees on the company's time. Others have gone, or are thinking of going, still further. After the Cambodian invasion of 1970, Polaroid Corporation urged its employees to send telegrams to their elected representatives expressing their own sentiments on the controversy. The company arranged to pay for the cost of one telegram for each employee and it did so in a way that would give it no knowledge of just what the employees' sentiments were. Lawrence S. Phillips, the president of the Phillips-Van Heusen Corporation which employs 13,000 people, says companies should give their workers two weeks of paid time off at elections to allow them to participate more fully in the political process. He is encouraging his fellow businessmen to adopt such an idea.

The modern organization, it is true, does not provide its members with the 24-hour-a-day association which has characterized residential communities in the past. But this is more of an asset than a liability. Democratic, sophisticated man cannot endure such a closed-in arrangement, at least not for very long. He demands security and serenity combined with challenge and change. Thus, the modern work organization as it is evolving seems to be the institution most capable of providing what modern man most desperately needs: shelter without walls.

Such is the target and such is the task of the administrative revolution.

BIBLIOGRAPHY

Alksnitis, Juris G., "Employee Participation in Policy Determination," unpublished paper, Northeastern University (Boston), Department of Political Science (1970).

Argyris, Chris, *Personality and Organization: The Conflict Between System and Individual*. New York: Harper & Row, Publishers, 1957.

Ashen, Melvin, "The Management of Ideas," *Harvard Business Review* (July–August, 1964).

Baumhart, Raymond, *Ethics in Business*. New York: Holt, Rinehart & Winston, Inc., 1968.

Bennis, Warren G., "Post-Bureaucratic Leadership," *Transaction* (July–August, 1968).

Berkley, George E., *The Democratic Policeman*. Boston: Beacon Press, 1969.

———, "The Myth of War Profiteering," *The New Republic* (December 20, 1969).

Berle, Adolph A., Jr., *The 20th Century Capitalist Revolution*. New York: Harcourt, Brace & World, Inc., 1954.

——— and Means, Gardner C., *The Modern Corporation and Private Property*. Revised Edition. Cleveland: Harcourt, Brace & World, Inc., 1967.

Blau, Peter M., *Bureaucracy in Modern Society*. New York: Random House, Inc., 1956.

Blythe, Ronald, *Akenfield*. New York: Random House, Inc., 1969.

Boulding, Kenneth E., *The Organizational Revolution: A Study in the Ethics of Economic Organization.* New York: Harper & Row, Publishers, 1953.

Brownstone, M., "The Canadian System of Government," *Canadian Public Administration Review* (Winter, 1968).

Bundy, McGeorge, *The Strength of Government.* Cambridge, Mass.: Harvard University Press, 1969.

Burch, Francis B., "Maryland's 'Action Program' in Consumer Protection," *State Government* (Summer, 1969).

Caiden, Gerald, "Coping with Turbulence: Israel's Administrative Experience," *Journal of Comparative Administration* (November, 1969).

Chapman, Brian, *The Profession of Government.* London: Oxford University Press, 1959.

Cleveland, Harlan, "Dinosaurs and Personal Freedom," *The Saturday Review* (February 28, 1959).

Committee on Economic Development, *Japan in the Free World Economy.* New York: 1963.

Crosland, C. A. R., *The Future of Socialism.* Revised Edition. New York: Schocken Books, 1963.

Debbasch, Charles, *l'administration au pouvoir.* Paris: Calmann-Levy, 1969.

Dickens, Charles, *Bleak House.*

Downs, Anthony *Inside Bureaucracy,* Boston: Little, Brown and Company, 1966.

Drew, Elizabeth, "HEW Grapples with PPBS," *The Public Interest* (Summer, 1967).

Drucker, Peter F., "A Conversation with Peter Drucker," *Careers Today* (Charter Issue, 1968).

————, ed., *Preparing Tomorrow's Business Leaders Today.* Englewood Cliffs, N.J.: Prentice-Hall, Inc., 1968.

————, *The Age of Discontinuity.* New York: Harper & Row, Publishers, 1968.

Farb, Peter, *Man's Rise to Civilization as Shown by the Indians of North America from Primeval Times to the Coming of the Industrial State.* New York: E. P. Dutton & Co., Inc., 1968.

Fisch, Gerald G., "Line-Staff Is Obsolete," *Harvard Business Review* (September–October, 1961).

Formwalt, Russel J., "How to Fight Consumer Resistance," *Salesman's Opportunity* (June, 1970).

Fortune, "Report from Moscow" (May, 1970).

Galbraith, John Kenneth, *The New Industrial State*. Boston: Houghton Mifflin Company, 1967.

Gellhorn, Walter, *Ombudsmen and Others*. Cambridge, Mass.: Harvard University Press, 1966.

Gorham, William, "PPBS: Notes of a Practitioner," *The Public Interest* (Summer, 1967).

Grant, J. Douglas, "The Offender as a Correctional Manpower Resource," in *Up from Poverty*, Frank Riessman, ed. New York: Harper & Row, Publishers, 1968.

Gruson, Claude, *Origine et Espoirs de la Planification Francaise*. Paris: Dunod, 1968.

Harrington, Alan, *Life in the Crystal Palace*. New York: Alfred A. Knopf, Inc., 1959.

Hirsch, Werner A., and Marcus, Morton G., "Some Benefit-Cost Considerations of Universal Junior College Education," *National Tax Journal* (March, 1966).

Hoffer, Eric, *The True Believer*. New York: Harper & Row, Publishers, 1951.

Hoos, Ida R., "Automation, Systems Engineering and Public Administration: Observations and Reflections on the California Experience," *Public Administration Review* (December, 1966).

Ide, Yoshimoni, "Administrative Reform and Innovation: The Japanese Case," *International Social Science Journal*, no. 1 (1969).

Jennings, Eugene, "Mobicentric Man," *Psychology Today* (June, 1970).

Kaufmann, Carl B., *Man Incorporate*. New York: Doubleday & Company, Inc., 1967.

Kaufman, Herbert, *The Forest Ranger*. Baltimore, Maryland: Johns Hopkins Press, 1960.

Kidron, Michael, *Western Capitalism Since the War*. London: Weidenfeld and Nicolson, 1968.

Kotlen, Philip, *Marketing Management: Analysis, Planning and Control.* Englewood Cliffs, N.J.: Prentice-Hall, Inc., 1967.

Kuriloff, Arthur H., "An Experiment in Management: Putting Theory Y to the Test," *Personnel* (November–December, 1963).

Levinson, Harry, *The Exceptional Executive: A Psychological Conception.* Cambridge, Mass.: Harvard University Press, 1968.

Levitt, Theodore, "The Johnson Treatment," *Harvard Business Review* (January–February, 1967).

Lindsay, John, *The City.* New York: W. W. Norton & Company, Inc., 1969.

Livingston, J. Sterling, "Pygmalion in Management," *Harvard Business Review* (July–August, 1969).

MacGregor, Douglas, *The Human Enterprise.* New York: McGraw-Hill Book Company, 1960.

————, *Leadership and Motivation* (essays of Douglas MacGregor edited by Warren G. Bennis and Edgar M. Schein with the collaboration of Caroline MacGregor). Cambridge, Mass.: The MIT Press, 1966.

————, *The Professional Manager.* New York: McGraw-Hill Book Company, 1967.

Marchal, Jean, and Ducros, Bernard, *The Distribution of National Income.* London: Macmillan & Co. Ltd., 1968.

Marshall, S. L. A., "Why the Israeli Army Wins," *Harper's* (October, 1958).

Melman, Seymour, "Industrial Efficiency Under Managerial vs. Cooperative Decision-Making: A Comparative Study of Manufacturing Enterprise in Israel." Paper available from the Cambridge Institute.

Mendell, Jay S., "The Case of the Straying Scientist," *Harvard Business Review* (July–August, 1969).

Miller, Ernest G., "The Impact of T-Groups on Managerial Behavior," *Public Administration Review* (May–June, 1970).

Myers, Charles A., *The Impact of Computers on Management.* Cambridge, Mass: MIT Press, 1964.

Myrdal, Gunnar, *Challenge to Affluence.* New York: Pantheon Books, Inc., 1963.

Pessemier, Edgar A., *New-Product Decisions: An Analytical Approach.* New York: McGraw-Hill Book Company, 1966.

Pieroth, Elmar, "Arbeitnehme Werden Kapitalisten," *Quick* (May 20, 1970).

Qu'est-ce Que La Participation? Foreword by Alain Peyrefitte. Paris: Plon, 1969.

Riker, William H., *The NLRB Examiner*. ICP Case Series, no. 15. Indianapolis, Indiana: The Bobbs-Merrill Co., Inc., 1951.

Roethlisberger, Fritz J., *Man-in-Organization: Essays of F. J. Roethlisberger*. Cambridge, Mass.: Belknap Press of Harvard University Press, 1968.

Roll, Eric, *The World After Keynes: An Examination of the Economic Order*. Frederick A. Praeger, New York, 1968.

Schick, Allen, "The Road to PPB: The Stages of Budget Reform," *Public Administration Review* (December, 1966).

Schonfield, Andrew, *Modern Capitalism*. London: Oxford University Press, 1965.

Silberman, Charles E., *The Myths of Automation*. New York: Harper & Row, Publishers, 1966.

Simon, Herbert A., *The Shape of Automation: For Men and Management*. New York: Harper & Row, Publishers, 1965.

Schlesinger, Arthur M., Jr., *A Thousand Days*. Boston: Houghton Mifflin Company, 1965.

Slater, Philip E., and Bennis, Warren G., "Democracy Is Inevitable" *Harvard Business Review* (March–April, 1964).

Der Spiegel (May 26, 1962) [Feature article on Japan].

Von Knoeringen, Waldemar, *Geplante Zukunft?* Hannover: Verlag für Literatur und Zeitgeschehen, 1968.

Ways, Max, "Antitrust in an Era of Radical Change," *Fortune*, 1967.

———, "More Power to Everybody," *Fortune* (May, 1970).

Weiss, E. B., "Watch for Coming Decline in Nation's Sales Force," *Advertising Age* (June 22, 1970).

INDEX